Introduction to Our NEAB Re~~vision Guid~~

Coordination Group Publications Ltd. was set up with the aim of
revision material for the National Curriculum. Following popular
our very successful Revision Guides for GCSE double science ar
a number of syllabus-specific versions for the NEAB and SEG dc

These brilliant NEAB Modular Science Revision Guides have <u>Three Top Features</u>:

Careful and Complete Explanations

*Unlike other revision guides, we do not restrict ourselves to a brief outline of the bare
essentials. Instead we work hard to give complete, concise and carefully written
details on each topic.*

Deliberate Use of Humour

*We consider the humour to be an essential part of our Revision Guides. It is there to
keep the reader interested and entertained, and we are certain that it greatly assists
their learning. (It is not however expected to win us any awards...)*

Carefully Matched to the NEAB Modular Syllabus, and more...

*We have taken great care to ensure that this book follows the exact detail of the NEAB
modular syllabus. Once again however we feel that merely illustrating the syllabus is
an inadequate approach. We have therefore done rather more than simply list the
basic syllabus details and add pictures. Instead we have endeavoured to include all the
relevant explanation which appears to us to be necessary.   The result is a full 96
pages giving a clear explanation of the whole syllabus content. We hope you will
appreciate the amount of time and care which has gone into this.*

---

*The early modules include material needed in the final exam. This material is contained
in blue boxes (like this one) throughout the Early Modules Revision Guide.*

Buy our books — they're ace

Final Exam   # Contents

Module Three   ## Environment

(3.1) *Adaptation and Competition* .... Population Size & Distribution 1
  "   "   "   .... Adapt and Survive 2
  "   "   "   .... Predators and Prey 3
(3.2) *Energy and Nutrient Transfer* .... Food Webs 4
  "   "   "   .... Making Holes in Food Webs 5
  "   "   "   .... Pyramids Of Number & Biomass 6
(3.3) *Nutrient Cycles* .... Decomposition & the Carbon Cycle 7
(3.4) *Human Impact on the Environment* ...... There's Too Many People 8
  "   "   "   "   .....Acid Rain 9
Revision Summary for Module Three 10

Module Four   ## Inheritance and Selection

(4.1) *Variation* .... Variation in Plants and Animals 11
(4.1) *Genetics and DNA* .... Genetics: Too Many Fancy Words 13
  "   "   .... Genes, Chromosomes and DNA 14
(4.2) *Cell Division* .... Sexual & Asexual Reproduction 15
(4.2) *Controlling Inheritance* .... Selective Breeding 16
(4.3) *Evolution* .... Evolution 17
  "   .... Fossils 18
(4.3/4.4) *Genetics and DNA* .... Mutations and Genetic Diseases 20
  "   "   "   .... X and Y Chromosomes 21
(4.5) *Hormones* .... Female Menstrual Cycle 22
Revision Summary for Module Four 23

Module Seven   ## Patterns of Chemical Change

(7.1) *Reaction Rates* .... Rates of Reaction 24
  "   "   .... Collision Theory 26
  "   "   .... Catalysts 28
(7.1) *Essentials Basics* .... Tests and Hazard Symbols 29
(7.2) *Reactions Involving Enzymes* .... Biological Catalysts 30
  "   "   "   .... Uses of Enzymes 31
(7.3) *Energy Transfer in Reactions* .... Energy Transfer in Reactions 32
(7.4) *Useful Products from Air* .... The Haber Process 33
  "   "   "   .... Fertiliser from Ammonia 34
(7.5) *Quantitative Chemistry* .... Relative Formula Mass 35
Revision Summary for Module Seven 36

Module Eight   ## Structures and Bonding

(8.1) *States of Matter* .... Solids, Liquids and Gases 37
  "   "   .... Changes of State 38
  "   "   .... Brownian Motion and Diffusion 39
(8.2) *Atomic Structure* .... Atoms 40
  "   "   .... Proton Number and Mass Number 41
  "   "   .... Electron Shells 42
(8.2) *Bonding* .... Elements, Compounds & Mixtures 43
  "   .... Ionic Bonding 44
  "   .... Electron Shells and Ions 45

(NEAB Syllabus reference)

Final Exam # *Contents*

(8.4) *Periodic Table* .... A History of The Periodic Table 46

     "   "   .... The Periodic Table 47

     "   "   .... Group O — The Noble Gases 48

     "   "   .... Group I — The Alkali Metals 49

     "   "   .... Reactions of the Alkali Metals 50

     "   "   .... Group VII — The Halogens 52

     "   "   .... Reactions of The Halogens 53

     "   "   .... Transition Metals 54

(8.6) *Compounds of Halogens* .... Industrial Salt 55

     "   "   .... Electrolysis of Salt 56

     "   "   .... Uses of Halogens 57

(8.7) *Representing Reactions* ....Chemical Equations 58

                                     Revision Summary for Module Eight 59

Module Eleven   ## *Forces*

(11.1) *Representing & Measuring Motion* ..... Velocity and Acceleration 60

     "   "   "   .... D-T and V-T Graphs 61

(11.2) *Forces and Acceleration* .... The Three Laws of Motion 62

     "   "   "   .... Mass, Weight and Gravity 64

     "   "   "   .... Force Diagrams 65

     "   "   "   .... Friction & Terminal Velocity 66

     "   "   "   .... Stopping Distances For Cars 67

(11.3) *Work done and Energy* .... Work Done and Kinetic Energy 68

(11.4) *Force and Pressure on Solids etc* .... Stretching Springs 69

     "   "   "   ...... Pressure on Surfaces 70

     "   "   "   ...... Pressure = Force / Area 71

(11.5) *The Solar System* .... The Cause of Days and Seasons 72

     "   "   "   .... The Solar System 73

     "   "   "   .... Satellites and Planets 74

(11.6) *The Universe* .... The Universe 75

                                     Revision Summary for Module Eleven 76

Module Twelve   ## *Waves and Radiation*

(12.1) *Characteristics of waves* .... Waves — Basic Principles 77

     "   "   .... Reflection 78

     "   "   .... Refraction 79

(12.2) *Characteristics of waves* .... Refraction: Two Special Cases 80

     "   "   .... Total Internal Reflection 81

(12.2) *The EM Spectrum* .... The EM Spectrum 82

(12.5) *Sound and Ultrasound* .... Sound Waves 84

     "   "   .... Frequency and Ultrasound 85

(12.3) *Types and Uses of Radiation* ....Types of Radiation 86

     "   "   "   ....Background Radiation 87

     "   "   "   ....Radiation Uses & Hazards 88

(12.4) *Atomic Structure* .... Atomic Structure 89

(NEAB Syllabus reference)   Revision Summary for Module Twelve 90

                                     Answers 90

                                     Index 91

Published by Coordination Group Publications Ltd.
Typesetting and Layout by The Coordination Group
Illustrations by: Sandy Gardner, e-mail: illustations@sandygardner.co.uk
and Bowser, Colorado USA

Coordinated by:
Paul Burton BSc (Hons)

Design Editors:
Chris Dennett BSc (Hons)
Theo Haywood BSc (Hons)

ISBN 1 84146 905 X

Groovy website: www.cgpbooks.co.uk

Printed by Elanders Hindson, Newcastle upon Tyne.
Clipart sources: CorelDRAW and VECTOR.
1199

Population Size & Distribution

Four Factors affect the Individual Organisms

These four physical factors fluctuate throughout the day and year. Organisms _live, grow_ and _reproduce_ in places where, and at times when, these conditions are suitable.

1) The _TEMPERATURE_ — this is rarely ideal for any organism.

2) The availability of _WATER_ — vital to all living organisms.

3) The _AMOUNT OF LIGHT AVAILABLE_ — this is most important to plants, but it also affects the visibility for animals.

4) _OXYGEN_ and _CARBON DIOXIDE_ — these affect respiration and photosynthesis respectively.

The Size of any Population depends on Five Factors

1) The _TOTAL AMOUNT OF FOOD_ or nutrients available.
2) The amount of _COMPETITION_ there is (from other species) for the same food or nutrients.
3) The _AMOUNT OF LIGHT AVAILABLE_ (this applies only to plants really).
4) The _NUMBER OF PREDATORS_ (or grazers) who may eat the animal (or plant) in question.
5) _DISEASE_.

All these factors help to explain why the _types_ of organisms vary from _place to place_ and from _time to time_.

The dynamics of plant and animal populations are really quite similar:
Plants often compete with each other for _space_, and for _water_ and _nutrients_ from the soil.
Animals often compete with each other for _space_, _food_ and _water_.

Generally organisms will thrive best if:

1) _THERE'S PLENTY OF THE GOOD THINGS IN LIFE_: food, water, space, shelter, light, etc.

2) _THEY'RE BETTER THAN THE COMPETITION AT GETTING IT_ (better _adapted_).

3) _THEY DON'T GET EATEN_.

4) _THEY DON'T GET ILL_.

That's pretty much the long and the short of it, wouldn't you say? So learn those four things. Every species is different, of course, but those _FOUR_ basic principles will always apply.

In Exam questions _YOU_ have to apply them to any new situation to work out what'll happen.

Revision stress — don't let it eat you up...

It's a strange topic is population sizes. In a way it seems like common sense, but it all seems to get so messy. Anyway, _learn all the points on this page_ and you'll be OK with it, I'd think.

Adapt and Survive

If you *learn the features* that make these animals and plants well adapted, you'll be able to apply them to any other similar creatures they might give you in the Exam.
Chances are you'll get a *camel*, *cactus* or *polar bear* anyway.

The Polar Bear — Designed for Arctic Conditions

The *Polar bear* has all these features: (which *many other arctic creatures* have too, so think on...)

1) *Large size* and *compact shape* (i.e. rounded), including dinky little ears, to keep the *surface area* to a *minimum* (compared to the body weight) — this all *reduces heat loss*.

2) A thick layer of *blubber* for *insulation* and also to survive hard times when food is scarce.

3) *Thick hairy coat* for keeping the body heat in.

4) *Greasy fur* which *sheds water* after swimming to *prevent cooling* due to evaporation.

5) *White fur* to match the surroundings for *camouflage*.

6) *Strong swimmer* to catch food in the water and *strong runner* to run down prey on land.

7) *Big feet* to *spread the weight* on snow and ice.

The Camel — Designed for Desert Conditions

The *camel* has all these features: (most of which are shared by *other desert creatures*...)

1) It can *store* a lot of *water* without problem. It can drink up to *20 gallons* at once.

2) It *loses very little water*. There's little *urine* and very little *sweating*.

3) It can tolerate *big changes* in its own *body temperature* to remove the need for sweating.

4) *Large feet* to *spread load* on soft sand.

5) All *fat* is stored in the *hump*, there is *no layer of body fat*. This helps it to *lose* body heat.

6) *Large surface area*. The shape of a camel is anything but compact, which gives it more surface area to *lose body heat* to its surroundings.

7) Its *sandy colour* gives good *camouflage*.

The Cactus is also Well Adapted for the Desert

1) It has *no leaves* — to *reduce water loss*.

2) It has a *small surface area* compared to its size which also *reduces water loss*. *(1000 x less than normal plants)*

3) It *stores water* in its thick stem.

4) *Spines* stop herbivores *eating* them.

5) *Shallow* but very extensive roots ensure water is *absorbed* quickly over a large area.

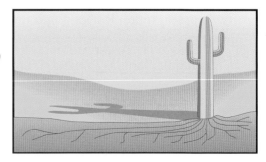

Predators and Prey

The Lion — a perfect Predator

1) _Strong_, _agile_ and _fast_.

2) _Strong jaws_ and _sharp teeth_ for killing prey.

3) Good _stereo vision_ with both eyes _facing forwards_.

4) _Camouflaged body_ for stalking prey.

5) The right sort of _teeth_ for _chewing meat_.

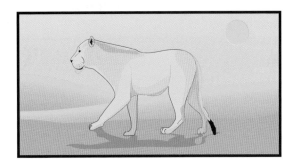

The Rabbit — a perfect Prey

1) _Fast_ and _agile_ for escaping capture.

2) Eyes on sides for _all-round vision_.

3) _Big ears_ for good hearing.

4) _Brown colour_ for _camouflage_.

5) _White tail_ to alert pals.

Populations of Prey and Predators go in Cycles

In a community containing prey and predators (as most of them do of course):

1) The _POPULATION_ of any species is usually _limited_ by the amount of _FOOD_ available.

2) If the population of the _PREY_ increases, then so will the population of the _PREDATORS_.

3) However as the population of predators _INCREASES_, the number of prey will _DECREASE_.

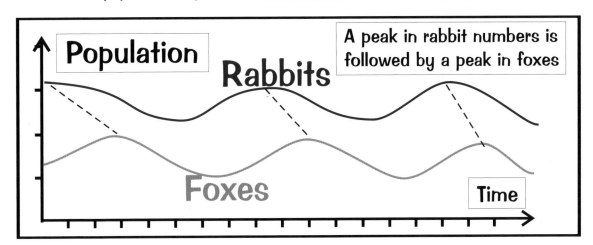

A peak in rabbit numbers is followed by a peak in foxes

i.e. _More grass_ means _more rabbits_. More rabbits means _more foxes_. But more foxes means fewer _rabbits_. Eventually fewer rabbits will mean _fewer foxes again_. This _up and down pattern_ continues...

Creature features — learn and survive...

It's worth learning all these survival features well enough to be able to write them down _from memory_. There's a whole world full of animals and plants, all with different survival features, but explaining them eventually becomes kinda "common sense", because the same principles tend to apply to them all.

4

Food Webs

A Woodland Food Web

Food webs are pretty easy really. Hideously easy in fact.

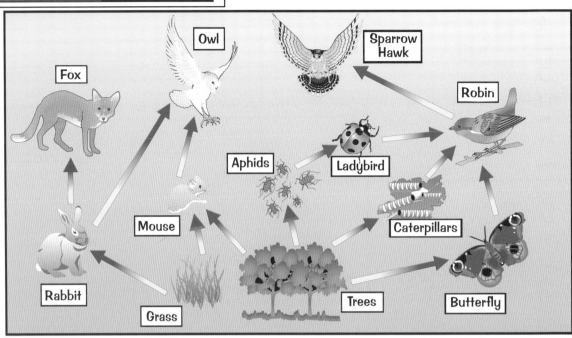

Food Chains — the Arrows show where the Energy goes

1) A *food chain* is just part of a *food web*, starting at the bottom and *following the arrows* up.
2) Remember, the *arrows* show which way the *food energy travels*.
3) Don't mix up *who eats who* either!
   The arrow means *"IS EATEN BY"*, so you *follow the arrow* to the one doing the *eating*.
4) From the woodland food web we could take this *food chain*:

Terminology you need to know

1) *PRODUCER* — all *plants* are *producers*. They use the Sun's energy to produce food energy.
2) *HERBIVORE* — animals which *only eat plants*, e.g. rabbits, caterpillars, aphids.
3) *CONSUMER* — all *animals* are *consumers*. All *plants* are *not*, because they are producers.
4) *PRIMARY CONSUMER* — animal which eats *producers* (plants).
5) *SECONDARY CONSUMER* — animal which eats primary consumers.
6) *CARNIVORE* — eats *only animals*, never plants.
7) *TOP CARNIVORE* — is *not eaten by anything else*, except decomposers after it dies.
8) *OMNIVORE* — eats *both plants and animals*.
9) *DECOMPOSER* — lives off all *dead material* — producers, consumers, top carnivore, the lot.

Learn about Food Webs, terminology and all...

That's got to be the prettiest food web ever drawn, wouldn't you say? Yeah well, anyway, the pretty pictures are the easy bit. It's those *9 definitions* which you really need to work at. That's what'll sort out the sheep from the goats in the Exam. So make sure you *know them all*.

Making Holes in Food Webs

A Typical Food Web for a Pond

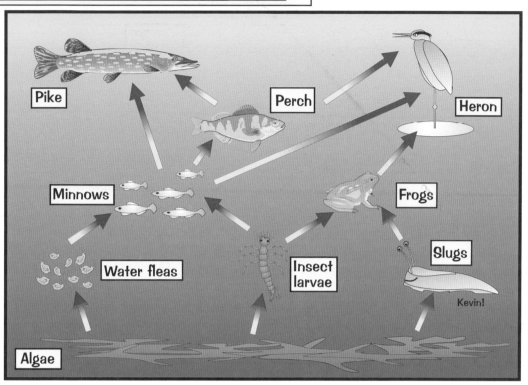

Pike

Perch

Heron

Minnows

Frogs

Water fleas

Insect larvae

Slugs

Kevin!

Algae

Exam Q. — What happens if you take out the frogs...?

1) This is the _usual Exam question_.
2) One of the animals is _wiped out_ — what effect will this have on the _other_ creatures?
3) For example, if all the _frogs_ were _removed_ what'd happen to the number of _slugs_ or _perch_?
4) It's _simple enough_, but you do have to _think it through_ fairly carefully:
   a) _SLUGS_ would _increase_ because there'd be _nothing to eat them_ now.
   b) _PERCH_ is a bit trickier. With no frogs the herons will get _hungry_ and so will _eat more perch_ (and minnows and insect larvae), so the perch will in fact _decrease_ in number.

You just have to understand the diagrams (i.e. who eats who) and think about it _real carefully_. Think about which animals _won't now get eaten_, and which animals _will go hungry_, and work out _what they'll do about it_ — and the effect that will have _on all the other things_ in the web.

Another Exam Q. — What if you took out the Minnows...?

1) First of all, _water fleas_ would _increase_.
2) _Perch_ on the other hand would be _really struggling_. They'd get _hungry_ for a start, but they'd also get _eaten_ a lot more _by pike_ and _heron_. Toughsky.
3) _Frogs_ would initially _benefit_ from _more insect larvae_ all to themselves, but would then suffer from _heron_ eating _more frogs_ due to there being _no minnows_ and fewer _perch_.
4) _Slugs_ would therefore _benefit_ because the _frogs_ would be eating more _insect larvae_ (instead of slugs) and also _getting eaten_ by heron. It's all real simple if you just _think it out_.

Learn about making holes in Food webs...

If they give you a food web question you can bet your very last fruit cake they're gonna want to wipe out one of the creatures and ask you what happens then. Practise with both these food webs by wiping out organisms (only one at a time!) and deciding what'll happen to the others.

Pyramids of Number & Biomass

This is hideously easy too. Just _make sure you know_ what _all_ the pyramids mean.

Each Level you go up, there's fewer of them...

_5000_ dandelions...   feed..   _100_ rabbits...   which feed....   _one_ fox.

IN OTHER WORDS, each time you go _up one level_ the _number of organisms goes down_ — _A LOT_.
It takes _a lot_ of food from the level _below_ to keep any one animal alive.
This gives us the good old _number pyramid_:

1 Fox
100 Rabbits
5,000 Dandelions

A typical pyramid of numbers

This is the _basic idea_ anyway. But there are cases where the pyramid is _not a pyramid at all_:

Number Pyramids Sometimes Look Wrong

This is a _pyramid_ except for the
top layer which goes _huge_:

500 Fleas
1 Fox
100 Rabbits
5,000 Dandelions

This is a _pyramid_ apart from the
bottom layer which is _way too small_:

1 Partridge
1000 Ladybirds
3,000 Aphids
1 Pear tree

Biomass Pyramids Never Look Wrong

When _number pyramids_ seem to go _wrong_ like this, then the good old _PYRAMID OF BIOMASS_
comes to the rescue. _Biomass_ is just how much all the creatures at each level would "_weigh_" if
you _put them all together_. So the _one pear tree_ would have a _big biomass_ and the _hundreds of
fleas_ would have _a very small biomass_. Biomass pyramids are _ALWAYS the right shape_:

Fleas
Fox
Rabbits
Dandelions

Partridge
Ladybirds
Aphids
Pear tree

Basically, _biomass pyramids_ are the only _sensible_ way to do it — it's just that _number pyramids_
are _easier to understand_.

Now Children, get your coloured wooden blocks out...

...hideously easy...

Decomposition & the Carbon Cycle

Another sixties pop group? Sadly not.

1) *Living things* are made of *materials* they take from the world around them.
2) When they *decompose*, ashes are returned to ashes, and dust to dust, as it were.
3) In other words *the elements they contain* are returned to the *soil* where they came from *originally*.
4) These elements are then *used by plants* to grow and the whole cycle *repeats* over and over again.

Decomposition *is carried out by Bacteria and Fungi*

1) All *plant matter* and *dead animals* are broken down (digested) by *microbes*.
2) This happens everywhere in *nature*, and also in *compost heaps* and *sewage works*.
3) All the important *elements* are thus *recycled*:
   Carbon, *Hydrogen*, *Oxygen* and *Nitrogen*.
4) The *ideal conditions* for creating *compost* are:
   a) *WARMTH*
   b) *MOISTURE*
   c) *OXYGEN (AIR)*
   d) *MICROBES* (i.e. *bacteria* and *fungi*)
   e) *ORGANIC MATTER* cut into *small pieces*.
      Make sure you *learn them* — *ALL FIVE*.

Extra microbes added (compost maker)

Finely shredded waste is best

Warmth generated by decomposition helps it all along

Mesh sides to let air in

There's a kid I know, and everyone calls him "the party mushroom". I'm not sure why really — they just say he's a fun guy to be with...

The Carbon Cycle Shows how Carbon is Recycled

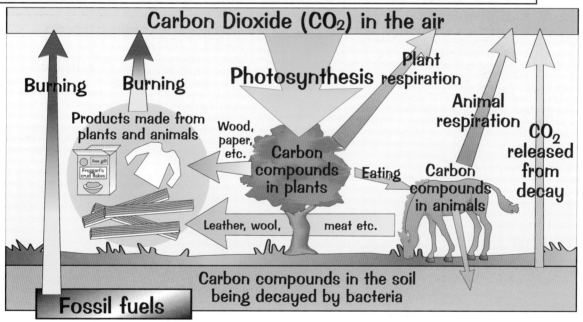

Carbon Dioxide (CO_2) in the air

Burning   Burning   Photosynthesis   Plant respiration   Animal respiration CO_2 released from decay

Products made from plants and animals

Wood, paper, etc.

Carbon compounds in plants

Eating

Carbon compounds in animals

free gift — Froggart's crud flakes

Leather, wool,   meat etc.

Carbon compounds in the soil being decayed by bacteria

Fossil fuels

This diagram isn't half as bad as it looks. *LEARN* these important points:
1) There's only *one arrow* going *DOWN*. The whole thing is "powered" by *photosynthesis*.
2) Both plant and animal *respiration* puts CO_2 *back into the atmosphere*.
3) *Plants* convert the carbon in CO_2 *from the air* into *fats*, *carbohydrates* and *proteins*.
4) These can then go *three ways*: be eaten, *decay* or be turned into *useful products* by man.
5) *Eating* transfers some of the fats, proteins and carbohydrates to *new* fats, carbohydrates and proteins *in the animal* doing the eating.
6) Ultimately these plant and animal products either *decay* or are *burned* and CO_2 *is released*.

On Ilkley Moor ba 'tat, On Ilkley Moor ba 'tat...

...where the dogs play football...

Learn the five ideal conditions for compost making. They like asking about that.
Sketch out your *own simplified version* of the carbon cycle, making sure it contains all the labels.
Practise *scribbling* it out *from memory*. And *keep trying till you can*.

There's Too Many People

There's One Born Every Minute — and it's Too Many

1) The *population of the world* is currently *rising out of control* as the graph shows.
2) This is mostly due to *modern medicine* which has stopped widespread death from *disease*.
3) It's also due to *modern farming methods* which can now provide the *food* needed for so many hungry mouths.
4) The *death rate* is now *much lower* than the *birth rate* in many under-developed countries.
   In other words there are *lots more babies born* than people *dying*.
5) This creates *big problems* for those countries trying to cope with all those extra people.
6) Even providing *basic health care* and *education* (about contraception!) is difficult, never mind finding them *places to live*, and *food to eat*.

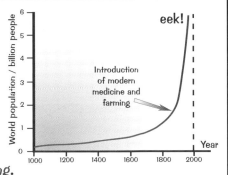

Increasing Living Standards Adds Even More Pressure

The rapidly increasing population is not the only pressure on the environment. The *increasing standard of living* amongst more *developed countries* also demands more from the environment. These *two* factors mean that:

1) Raw materials, including *non-renewable energy resources*, are rapidly being used up;
2) *more and more waste* is being produced;
3) unless waste is properly handled *more pollution* will be caused.

When the Earth's population was much smaller, the effects of human activity were usually small and local.

More People Means Less Land for Plants and Animals

There are *four* main ways that humans *reduce* the amount of land available for other *animals* and *plants*.

1) *Building*

2) *Farming*

3) *Dumping Waste*

4) *Quarrying*

More People Means More Environmental Damage

Human activity can pollute all three parts of the environment:
1) *Water* – with sewage, fertiliser and toxic chemicals;
2) *Air* – with smoke and gases such as sulphur dioxide;
3) *Land* – with toxic chemicals, such as pesticides and herbicides.
   These may then be washed from the land into water.

Learn the facts first — then you can build your rocket...

It's real scary innit — the way that graph of world population seems to be pointing nearly vertically upwards... tricky. Anyway, you just worry about your Exams instead, and make sure you learn all the grim facts. Four sections — *mini-essays* for each, *till you know it all*.

Acid Rain

Burning Fossil Fuels Causes Acid Rain

1) When _fossil fuels_ are _burned_ they release mostly _carbon dioxide_ which is causing the _Greenhouse Effect_. They also release _two_ other _harmful gases_: a) __SULPHUR DIOXIDE__
   b) various __NITROGEN OXIDES__

2) When these _mix with clouds_ they form _acids_. This then falls as _acid rain_.

3) _Cars_ and _power stations_ are the _main causes_ of acid rain.

Acid Rain Kills Fish, Trees and Statues

1) Acid rain causes _lakes_ to become _acidic_ which has a _severe effect_ on its _ecosystem_.
2) The way this happens is that the acid causes _aluminium salts_ to _dissolve_ into the water. The resulting _aluminium ions_ are _poisonous_ to many _fish and birds_.
3) Acid rain kills _trees_.
4) Acid rain _damages limestone buildings_ and _ruins stone statues_.

Acid Rain is Prevented by Cleaning up Emissions

1) _Power stations_ now have _Acid Gas Scrubbers_ to take the harmful gases _out_ before they release their fumes into the atmosphere.
2) _Cars_ are now being fitted with _catalytic converters_ to clean up their _exhaust gases_.
3) The other way of reducing acid rain is simply to _reduce our usage_ of _fossil fuels_.

Catalytic converter

Learn about Acid Rain — and always take a coat...

There aren't too many details on acid rain. If you can't learn all this lot properly then you're just not trying. Don't forget they won't ask you easy stuff like "Is acid rain caused by cars or monkeys?", they'll test you on trickier stuff like "Which gases cause acid rain and why?". _Learn and enjoy._ And _smile_. ☺

Revision Summary for Module Three

There's a lot of words in Module Three. Most topics are pretty waffly with a lot of drivelly facts, and it can be real hard to learn them all. But learn them you must. You need to practise scribbling down what you can remember on each topic, and then checking back to see what you missed. These questions give you a pretty good idea of what you should know. You need to practise and practise them — till you can float through them all, like a cloud or something.

1) Name the four factors that affect individual organisms on a daily basis.
2) What are the *five* basic things which determine the size of a population of a species?
3) List seven survival features of the polar bear and of the camel.
4) List five survival features for the cactus.
5) Give five survival features for the lion and for the rabbit.
6) Sketch a graph of prey and predator populations and explain the shapes.
7) Describe what food chains and food webs are. Give two examples of both.
8) Write down the 9 technical terms for food webs (P.4) and give a definition of each one.
9) What is the basic approach to questions which make holes in food webs?
10) What is happening to the world population? What is largely responsible for this trend?
11) What are number pyramids? Why do you generally get a pyramid of numbers?
12) Why do number pyramids sometimes go wrong, and which pyramids are always right?
13) Which two organisms are responsible for the decay of organic matter?
14) What are the five ideal conditions for making compost? Draw a compost maker.

15) What is the Carbon Cycle all to do with? Copy and fill in as much of it from memory as you can.
16) What problems does a rapidly increasing population create for a country?
17) What are the four main ways humans reduce the land available for other plants and animals.
18) What effect does the ever-increasing number of people have on the environment?
19) Which two gases are the biggest cause of the greenhouse effect?
20) Explain how the greenhouse effect happens. What dire consequences could there be?
21) What is causing the rise in levels of each the two problem gases. What is the solution?
22) Which gases cause acid rain? Where do these gases come from?
23) What are the three main harmful effects of acid rain? Explain exactly how fish are killed.
24) Give three ways that acid rain can be reduced.
25) What are the three main sources of atmospheric pollution?
26) What are the precise environmental effects of each of these three sources of pollution?

Variation in Plants and Animals

1) Young plants and animals obviously _resemble_ their _parents_. In other words they show _similar characteristics_ such as jagged leaves or perfect eyebrows.

2) However young animals and plants can also _differ_ from their parents and each other.

3) These similarities and differences lead to _variation_ within the same species.

4) The word _"VARIATION"_ sounds far too fancy for its own good. All it means is how animals or plants of the same species _look or behave_ slightly different from each other. You know, a bit _taller_ or a bit _fatter_ or a bit more _scary-to-look-at_ etc.

There are _two_ causes of variation: _Genetic Variation_ and _Environmental Variation_.

Read on, and learn...

1) Genetic variation

You'll know this already.

1) _All animals_ (including humans) are bound to be _slightly different_ from each other because their _GENES_ are slightly different.

2) Genes are the code inside all your cells which determine how your body turns out. We all end up with a slightly different set of genes.

3) The _exceptions_ to that rule are _identical twins_, because their genes are _exactly the same_.

But even identical twins are never _completely identical_ — and that's because of the other factor:

2) Environmental Variation is shown up by Twins

If you're not sure what _"environment"_ means, think of it as _"upbringing"_ instead — it's pretty much the same thing — how and where you were "brought up".

Since we know the _twins' genes_ are _identical_, any differences between them _must_ be caused by slight differences _in their environment_ throughout their lives.

Twins give us a fairly good idea of how important the _two factors_ (genes and environment) are, _compared to each other_, at least for animals — plants always show much _greater variation_ due to differences in their environment than animals do, as explained below.

Environmental Variation in Plants is much Greater

PLANTS are _strongly affected_ by:
1) _Temperature_
2) _Sunlight_
3) _Moisture level_
4) _Soil composition_

For example, plants may grow _twice as big_ or _twice as fast_ due to _fairly modest_ changes in environment such as the amount of _sunlight_ or _rainfall_ they're getting, or how _warm_ it is or what the _soil_ is like.

A cat, on the other hand, born and bred in the North of Scotland, could be sent out to live in equatorial Africa and would show no significant changes — it would look the same, eat the same, and it would probably still puke up everywhere.

Variation in Plants and Animals

Environmental Variation in Animals

Stubborn cats notwithstanding...

In Exams they do like questions on *the* effects of *environment on animals*.

Typically, they'll ask you *which features* of a human or a pet *MIGHT be affected* by their environment (i.e. the way they were "brought up").

In fact, *almost every single aspect* of a human (or animal) will be affected by *upbringing* in some way, however small, and in fact it's considerably easier to list the very few factors that *aren't* affected by environment and these are they:

4 Animal Characteristics NOT affected at all by Environment:

1) *EYE COLOUR*.

2) *HAIR COLOUR* in most animals (but not humans where vanity plays a big part).

3) *INHERITED DISEASES* like haemophilia, cystic fibrosis, etc.

4) *BLOOD GROUP*.

And that's about it! So *learn those four* in case they ask you.

Combinations of Genetic and Environmental Variation

EVERYTHING ELSE is determined by *A MIXTURE* of *genetic* and *environmental* factors: *Body weight*, *height*, *skin colour*, *condition of teeth*, *academic or athletic prowess*, etc. etc.

The *tricky* bit is working out just *how significant* environmental factors are for all these other features.

For example...

...imagine you got mixed up with another baby at the hospital and had grown up in a *totally different household* from your own. How different would you be now?   It's not at all easy to tell how much of your *physique* and (more importantly) your *personality* are due to *genes* and how much to *upbringing* (*environment*).   It's a big social issue, so it is.

Don't let Everything get to you — just learn the facts...

There are six sections on these two pages. After you think you've learnt it all, *cover the pages* and do a "*mini-essay*" on each of the six sections. Then *check back* and see what important points you missed. The coloured ink highlights the important bits.

Genetics: Too Many Fancy Words

When it comes to _big fancy words_ then _Biology_ is the subject where it's all happening.
And _genetics_ is the topic that _REALLY_ walks away with all the prizes.
It seems _hard to believe_ that so many exceptionally cumbersome, excessively complicated and virtually unintelligible words can conceivably be necessary, or indeed be particularly desirable...

Here's a summary of all the fancy words used in _genetics_ with an explanation of what they actually mean. It really does make a _big difference_ if you _learn_ these first. It's very difficult to understand _anything_ in genetics if you don't actually know what half the words mean.

DNA — is the _molecule_ which contains _genes_. It's shaped like a _double helix_ (a spiral).

Chromosomes — are those funny _X-shaped_ things that are found in the _cell nucleus_. The arms are made up of _very long coils of DNA_, so chromosomes also contain _genes_.

Gene — is a _section of DNA molecule_. It's also part of the _arm_ of a chromosome.

Allele — is a _gene_ too. When you have _two different versions_ of the same gene you have to call them _alleles_ instead of genes. (It _is_ more sensible than it sounds.)

Dominant — this refers to an _allele_ or _gene_. The dominant allele is the one which will _determine_ the characteristic which appears. _It dominates the recessive allele_ on the other chromosome.

Recessive — is the _allele_ which does _not_ usually affect how the organism turns out because it's _dominated_ by the dominant allele (fairly obviously).

Sexual Reproduction — Involves the fusion of male _and_ female gametes (sex cells). Because there are two parents, the offspring contains _a mixture of their parent genes_.

Asexual Reproduction — Involves _only one_ parent, and the offspring therefore have _exactly the same genes as the parent_ (i.e. they're clones).

Mitosis — is the process of _cell division_ where one cell splits into _two identical cells_.

Gamete — is either a _sperm cell_ or an _egg cell_. All _gametes_ have half the number of chromosomes of a body cell.

Zygote — is the delightful name given to each newly-formed human life, just after the (equally delightfully-named) _gametes_ _fuse together_ at fertilisation.

You'd think they could have come up with some slightly prettier names, as would befit this most awesome and wonderful moment, really. Your whole life, that great voyage of discovery and wonder, of emotion and reason, of conscience and consciousness, begins with that fateful and magical moment when...
..."two GAMETES fuse to form a ZYGOTE"...   _Ahh, what poetry..._

Too many fancy words, but you still gotta learn 'em...

Practise by covering up the right hand side of the page and scribbling down a description for each word. That's nice and easy. Just keep looking back and practising _till you can do them all_.

Genes, Chromosomes and DNA

If you're going to get _anywhere_ with this topic you definitely need to learn these confusing words and exactly what they mean. You have to _make sure you know_ exactly what _DNA_ is, what and where _chromosomes_ are, and what and where a _gene_ is. If you don't get that sorted out first, then anything else you read about them won't make a lot of sense to you — _will it?_

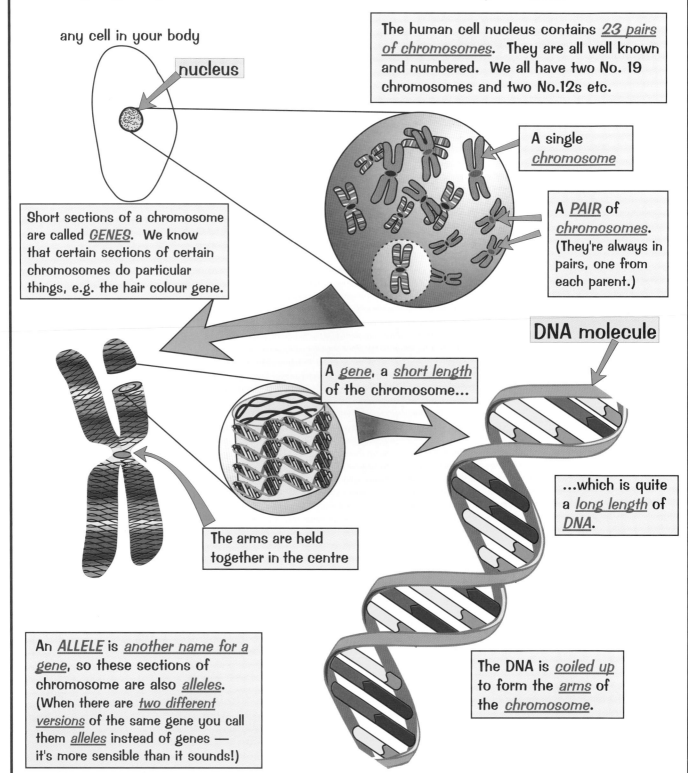

any cell in your body

nucleus

The human cell nucleus contains _23 pairs of chromosomes_. They are all well known and numbered. We all have two No. 19 chromosomes and two No.12s etc.

A single _chromosome_

A _PAIR_ of _chromosomes_. (They're always in pairs, one from each parent.)

Short sections of a chromosome are called _GENES_. We know that certain sections of certain chromosomes do particular things, e.g. the hair colour gene.

DNA molecule

A _gene_, a _short length_ of the chromosome...

...which is quite a _long length_ of _DNA_.

The arms are held together in the centre

The DNA is _coiled up_ to form the _arms_ of the _chromosome_.

An _ALLELE_ is _another name for a gene_, so these sections of chromosome are also _alleles_. (When there are _two different versions_ of the same gene you call them _alleles_ instead of genes — it's more sensible than it sounds!)

Hard Learning? — don't blow it all out of proportion...

This is a real easy page to learn, don't you think. Why, you could learn the whole thing with both ears tied behind your head. _Cover the page_ and _scribble down_ all the diagrams and details.

Sexual & Asexual Reproduction

Sexual Reproduction

Fertilisation:

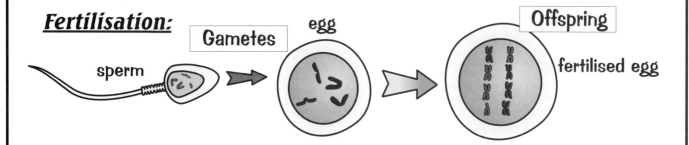

sperm — Gametes — egg — Offspring — fertilised egg

> **SEXUAL REPRODUCTION** involves the fusion of male and female gametes (sex cells). Because there are **TWO** parents, the offspring contains *a mixture of their parents genes*.

The offspring will receive its *outward characteristics* as a *mixture* from the two sets of chromosomes, so it will *inherit features* from *both parents*. This is why *sexual* reproduction produces more variation than *asexual* reproduction. Pretty cool, eh.

Asexual Reproduction

ORDINARY CELL DIVISION produces new cells *identical* to the original cell. This is how all plants and animals *grow* and produce *replacement cells*. Cells throughout our body *divide* and *multiply* by this process. However some organisms also *reproduce* using ordinary cell division, *bacteria* being a good example. This is known as *asexual* reproduction. Here is a *DEFINITION* of it, for you to learn:

> In **ASEXUAL REPRODUCTION** there is only **ONE** parent, and the offspring therefore have *exactly the same genes* as the parent (i.e. they're clones).

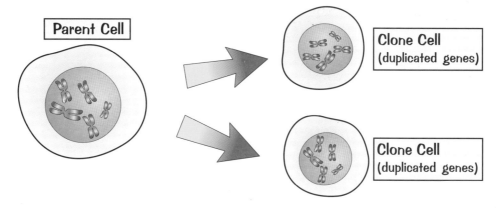

Parent Cell — Clone Cell (duplicated genes) — Clone Cell (duplicated genes)

This is because all the cells *in both parent and offspring* were produced by *ordinary cell division*, so they must all have *identical genes* in their cell nuclei. Asexual reproduction therefore produces no variation. Some *plants* reproduce asexually, e.g. potatoes, strawberries and daffodils.

Now that I have your undivided attention...

You need to *learn* the definition of *sexual reproduction* and the sequence of diagrams, and also the definition of *asexual reproduction*. Now *cover the page* and *scribble down* the two definitions and sketch out the sequence of diagrams — *don't waste time* with neatness — just find out if you've *learnt it all* yet.

Selective Breeding

Selective Breeding is Very Simple

SELECTIVE BREEDING is also called _artificial selection_, because humans artificially select the plants or animals that are going to breed and flourish, according to what _WE_ want from them. This is the basic process involved in selective breeding:

1) From your existing stock select the ones which have the _BEST CHARACTERISTICS_.
2) _Breed them_ with each other.
3) Select the _best_ of the _OFFSPRING_, and combine them with the best that you already have and _breed again_.
4) Continue this process over _SEVERAL GENERATIONS_ to _develop_ the _desired traits_.

Selective Breeding is Very Useful in Farming

Artificial Selection like this is used in _most areas of modern farming_, to great benefit:

1) Better BEEF

Selectively breeding _beef cattle_ to get the _best beef_ (taste, texture, appearance, etc.).

2) Better MILK

Selectively breeding _milking cows_ to increase _milk yield_ and _resistance to disease_.

3) Better CHICKENS

Selectively breeding _chickens_ to improve _egg size_ and _number of eggs_ per hen.

4) Better FLOWERS

Selectively breeding _flowers_ to produce _bigger_ and _better_ and _more colourful ones_.

5) Better WHEAT

Selectively breeding _wheat_ to produce new varieties with better _yields_ and better _disease-resistance_ too.

Don't sit there brooding over it, just learn the info...

Selective breeding is a very simple topic. In the Exam they'll likely give you half a page explaining how a farmer in Sussex did this or that with his crops or cows, and then they'll suddenly ask: "What is meant by selective breeding". That's when you just write down the four points at the top of this page. Then they'll ask you to "_Suggest other ways that selective breeding might be used by farmers in Sussex to improve their yield_". That's when you just list some of the examples that you've learnt.

Evolution

The Theory of Evolution is Cool

1) This suggests that all the animals and plants on Earth gradually "*evolved*" over *millions of years*, rather than just suddenly popping into existence. Makes sense.

2) Life on Earth began as *simple organisms living in water* and gradually everything else evolved from there. And it only took about *3,000,000,000 years*.

Fossils *Provide* Evidence *for it*

1) *Fossils* provide lots of *evidence* for evolution.
2) They show how today's species have *changed and developed* over *millions of years*.
3) There are quite a few "*missing links*" though because the fossil record is *incomplete*.
4) This is because *very very few* dead plants or animals actually turn into fossils.
5) Most just *decay away* completely.

The Evolution of The Horse is Ace

1) One set of fossils which *is* pretty good though is that showing *the evolution of the horse*.
2) This developed from quite a small creature about the size of a *dog* and the fossils show how the *middle toe* slowly became bigger and bigger and eventually evolved into the familiar *hoof* of today's horse.
3) It took about *60 million years* though.
4) This is *pretty strong evidence* in support of *evolution* because it really shows evolution happening!

Forefeet	Evolution of the horse

Hyracotherium

Mesohippus

Merychippus

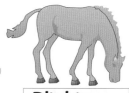

Pliohippus

Modern

Extinction *is Pretty Bad News*

The *dinosaurs* and *hairy mammoths* became *EXTINCT* and it's only *FOSSILS* that tell us they ever existed at all, (notwithstanding the odd questionable glacier story).

There are *THREE WAYS* a species can become *EXTINCT*:
1) The *ENVIRONMENT CHANGES* too quickly.
2) A new *PREDATOR* or *DISEASE* kills them all.
3) They can't *COMPETE* with another (new) species for *FOOD*.

As the environment *slowly changes*, it will gradually favour certain new characteristics amongst the members of the species and over many generations those features will *proliferate*. In this way, the species *constantly adapts* to its changing environment. But if the environment changes *too fast* the whole species may be *wiped out*, i.e. *extinction*...

Stop horsing around and just learn the facts...

Another stupefyingly easy page to learn. Use the *mini-essay* method. Just make sure you *learn every fact*, that's all. Dinosaurs never did proper revision and look what happened to them. (Mind you they did last about 200 million years, which is about 199.9 million more than we have, so far...)

Fossils

FOSSILS are the "_remains_" of plants and animals which lived _millions of years ago_.

There are Three ways that Fossils can be Formed:

1) From the _hard parts_ of animals.
2) From the _softer parts_ of plants or animals.
3) When _no decay_ happens at all.

1) _Fossils Usually Form from the Hard Parts of animals:_

1) It's usually the hardest parts of animals like _bones_, _teeth_, _shells_, etc., which eventually become fossils.

2) That's because these things don't _don't decay_ easily, so they tend to last a long time when _buried_.

3) Eventually they are _replaced by minerals_ as they decay, forming a _rock-like substance_ shaped like the original hard part.

4) The surrounding sediment also turns to rock, but the fossil stays _distinct_ inside until eventually someone _digs it up_.

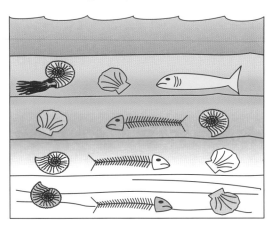

2) _Fossils Can Form from Softer Parts of animals:_

1) Sometimes fossils are formed from the _softer parts_ which somehow haven't decayed.

2) The soft material gradually becomes _"petrified"_ (turns to stone) as it slowly decays and is _replaced by minerals_.

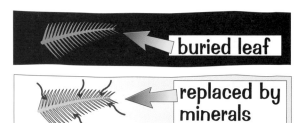

buried leaf

replaced by minerals

3) This is _rare_, since there are _very few occasions_ when decay occurs so _slowly_.

4) Most _plant fossils_ are of this type because plants are generally _soft_ and _decay quickly_.

5) For _petrification_ to happen, the plant or animal usually has to fall into a _swamp or bog_ and be covered quickly.

6) If there is virtually _no oxygen_ reaching the plant it will not decay quickly, and _petrification_ can gradually take place.

Fossils

3) *In Places Where No Decay Happens:*

Where no decay whatsoever happens, then the *whole original plant or animal* may survive for *thousands of years*. There are **THREE IMPORTANT EXAMPLES:**

a) *AMBER* — no *OXYGEN* or *MOISTURE* for the *decay microbes*.

INSECTS are often found *fully preserved* in amber, which is a clear yellow "stone" made of *FOSSILISED RESIN* that ran out of an ancient tree hundreds of millions of years ago, engulfing the insect.

b) *GLACIERS* — too *COLD* for the *decay microbes* to work.

A *HAIRY MAMMOTH* was found fully preserved in a glacier somewhere several years ago.

(at least that's what I heard, though I never saw any pictures of it so maybe it was a hoax, I'm not really sure, but anyway in principle one could turn up any time...)

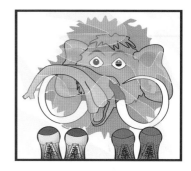

c) *WATERLOGGED BOGS* — too *ACIDIC* for *decay microbes*.

A *10,000 year old man* was found in a bog a few years ago. He was dead, and a bit squashed but otherwise quite well preserved, although it was clear he had been *murdered*.

(Police are not looking for witnesses and have asked anyone *else* who thinks they may have important information to just keep away.)

Evidence from Rock and Soil Strata

The fossils found in *rock layers* tell us *TWO THINGS*:

1) What the creatures and plants *LOOKED LIKE*.

2) *HOW LONG AGO THEY EXISTED*, by the type of rock they're in.

Generally speaking, the *DEEPER* you find the fossil, the *OLDER* it will be, though of course rocks get pushed upwards and eroded, so very old rocks can become exposed.

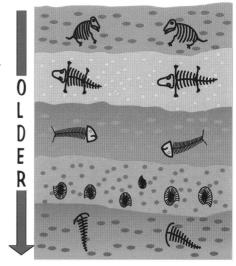

Fossils are usually *dated* by geologists who *ALREADY KNOW THE AGE OF THE ROCK*. The Grand Canyon in Arizona is about *1 mile deep*. It was formed by a river slowly cutting down through layers of rock. The rocks at the bottom are about *1,000,000,000 years old*, and the fossil record in the sides is pretty cool.

Don't get bogged down in all this information...

Make sure you're fully aware of the *three* different types of *fossil* and how they're *formed*. Also make sure you learn all the details about what information rocks provide. Many people read stuff and then think they know it. It's only if you *cover it up* that you find out what you *really* know.

Mutations and Genetic Diseases

A MUTATION occurs when an organism develops with some _strange new characteristic_ that no other member of the species has had before. For example if someone was born with blue hair it would be caused by a mutation. Some mutations are beneficial, but _most are disastrous_ (e.g. blue hair).

Radiation and Certain Chemicals cause Mutations

Mutations occur 'naturally', probably caused by "natural" background radiation (from the sun, and rocks etc.) or just the laws of chance that every now and then the DNA doesn't quite copy itself properly. However _the chance of mutation is increased_ by exposing yourself:

1) to _ionising radiation_, including _X-rays_ and _Ultra-Violet light_, (which are the highest-frequency parts of the _EM spectrum_) together with radiation from _radioactive substances_. For each of these examples, the _greater_ the _dose_ of radiation, the _greater_ the _chance_ of mutation.

No no! not me!

2) to certain _chemicals_ which are known to cause mutations. Such chemicals are called _mutagens_. If the mutations produce cancer then the chemicals are often called _carcinogens_. Cigarette smoke contains chemical mutagens (or carcinogens).

Genetic Diseases

There are only two genetic diseases that you need to know:

1) Cystic Fibrosis is caused by a Defective Gene

1) _CYSTIC FIBROSIS_ is a _GENETIC DISEASE_ which affects about _1 in 1600 people_ in the UK.

2) It's a disorder of the _cell membranes_ caused by a _defective gene_.

3) _Both_ parents must have the defective gene for the disorder to be passed on although both may be _carriers_. A carrier is somebody who has the _defective gene_ without actually having the _disorder_.

4) The result of the _defective gene_ is that the body produces a lot of thick sticky mucus in the lungs, which has to be removed by _massage_.

5) Excess mucus also occurs in the _pancreas_, causing _digestive problems_.

6) Much more seriously though, _THE BLOCKAGE OF THE AIR PASSAGES_ in the lungs causes a lot of _CHEST INFECTIONS_. There's still _no cure_ or effective treatment for this condition.

7) _Physiotherapy and antibiotics_ clear them up but slowly the sufferer becomes more and more ill.

2) Huntington's Chorea is caused by a Dominant Allele

1) This is a disorder of the _nervous system_ that isn't nice, resulting in shaking, erratic body movements and severe mental deterioration.

2) The disorder can be inherited from _one parent_ who has the disorder.

Don't get your genes in a twist, this stuff's easy...

There are three sections with numbered points for each. _Memorise_ the headings and learn the numbered points, then _cover the page_ and _scribble down_ everything you can remember. I know it makes your head hurt, but every time you try to remember the stuff, the more it sinks in. It'll all be worth it in the end.

X and Y Chromosomes

There are _23 matched pairs_ of chromosomes in every human body cell. You'll notice the 23rd pair are labelled XY. They're the two chromosomes that _decide whether you turn out male or female_. They're called the **X** and **Y** chromosomes because they look like an **X** and a **Y**.

> _ALL MEN_ have _an X_ and _a Y_ chromosome: XY
> _The Y chromosome is DOMINANT_ and causes _male characteristics_.
>
> _ALL WOMEN_ have _two X chromosomes_: XX
> The **XX** combination allows _female characteristics_ to develop.

The diagram below shows the way the male XY chromosomes and female XX chromosomes _split up to form the gametes_ (eggs or sperm), and then _combine together at fertilisation_.
  The criss cross lines show all the _possible_ ways the X and Y chromosomes _could_ combine. Remember, _only one of these_ would actually happen for any offspring.
What the diagram shows us is the _RELATIVE PROBABILITY_ of each type of zygote (offspring) occurring.

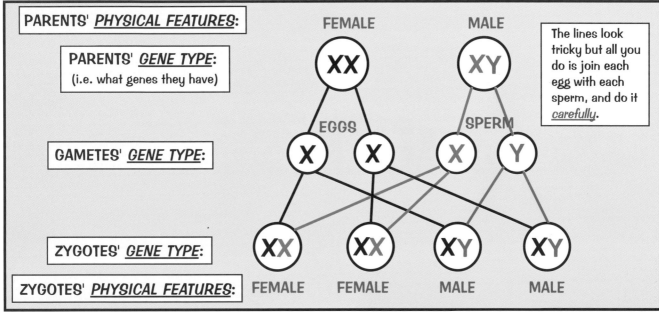

PARENTS' _PHYSICAL FEATURES_:

PARENTS' _GENE TYPE_:
(i.e. what genes they have)

GAMETES' _GENE TYPE_:

ZYGOTES' _GENE TYPE_:

ZYGOTES' _PHYSICAL FEATURES_: FEMALE   FEMALE   MALE   MALE

The lines look tricky but all you do is join each egg with each sperm, and do it _carefully_.

The other way of doing this is with a _checkerboard_ type diagram. If you don't understand how it works, ask "Teach" to explain it. The _pairs of letters_ in the middle show the _gene types_ of the possible offspring.

Both diagrams show that there'll be the _same proportion_ of _male and female offspring_, because there are _two XX results_ and _two XY results_.

Don't forget that this _50:50 ratio_ is only a _probability_. If you had four kids they _could_ all be _boys_ — yes I know, terrifying isn't it?

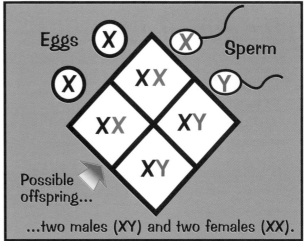

...two males (XY) and two females (XX).

How can it take all that just to say it's a 50:50 chance...

Make sure you know all about X and Y chromosomes and who has what combination.
The diagrams are real important. Practise reproducing them until you can do it _effortlessly_.

Female Menstrual Cycle

1) The _monthly_ release of an _egg_ from a womens _ovaries_ and the build up and break down of a protective lining in the _womb_ is called the _menstrual cycle_.

2) _Hormones_ released by the _pituitary gland_ and the _ovaries_ control the different stages of the menstrual cycle.

The Menstrual Cycle has Four Stages

STAGE 1   _Day 1 is when the bleeding starts._ The uterus lining breaks down for about four days.

STAGE 2   _The lining of the womb builds up again_, from day 4 to day 14, into a thick spongy layer of blood vessels ready to receive a fertilised egg.

STAGE 3   _An egg is developed and then released_ from the ovary at day 14.

STAGE 4   _The wall is then maintained_ for about 14 days, until day 28.   If no fertilised egg has landed on the uterus wall by day 28 then the spongy lining starts to break down again and the whole cycle starts over. The diagram below illustrates this.

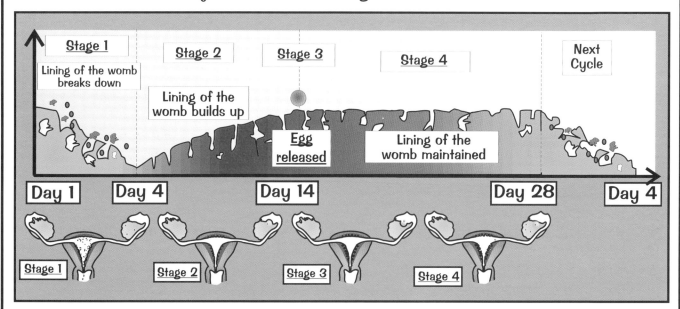

The control of Fertility

Women who want to control their fertility can be given extra doses of hormones involved in the menstrual cycle.

1) _FERTILITY DRUGS_ contain hormones that _stimulate_ the release of the egg from the ovaries. But you do have to be _careful_ with the _dosage_ of these drugs or too many eggs can be released resulting in _multiple births_.

2) _CONTRACEPTIVE DRUGS_ contain hormones that _prevent_ the release of eggs from the ovaries. These also have their _drawbacks_ as the hormones can produce _side-effects_ such as headaches and nausea. They are also _not_ 100% effective at preventing pregnancy.

Female or otherwise, you've still gotta learn it...

This is the relatively simple stuff on the menstrual cycle and it's definitely well worth learning. Make sure you know what the hormones do and where they are produced, and also how hormones are used to control fertility.   _Learn and enjoy._

Revision Summary for Module Four

Gee, all that business about genes and chromosomes and the like — it's all pretty serious stuff, don't you think? It takes a real effort to get your head round it all. There's too many big fancy words, for one thing. But there you go — life's tough and you've just gotta face up to it. Use these questions to find out what you know — and what you don't. Then look back and learn the bits you didn't know. Then try the questions again, and again...

1) What are the two types of variation? Describe their relative importance for plants and animals.
2) Name the four factors affecting environmental variation in plants.
3) What causes the small differences between "identical" twins?
4) List four features of animals which aren't affected at all by environment, and four which are.
5) On P. 13 there are 11 fancy words to do with genetics. List them all — with explanations.
6) What is the main difference between asexual and sexual reproduction?
7) What is the difference between a dominant and a recessive gene?
8) Draw a set of diagrams showing the relationship between: cell, nucleus, chromosomes, genes, DNA.
9) What is asexual reproduction? Give a proper definition for it.
10) What is sexual reproduction? Give a proper definition for it.
11) Describe the basic procedure in selective breeding (of cows). Give five other examples.
12) What is meant by selective breeding?
13) Give details about the theory of evolution. Give evidence for the theory.
14) Describe three ways that a species can become extinct.
15) Describe fully the three ways that fossils can form. Give examples of each type.
16) Describe three places where no decay occurs. Explain why there is no decay.
17) Explain how fossils found in rocks support the theory of evolution. Refer to the horse.
18) Describe how radiation causes mutations. What else can causes mutations?
19) Name three things that increase the chance of a mutation occurring.
20) List the symptoms and treatment of cystic fibrosis. What causes this disease?
21) Explain the grim odds for Huntington's Chorea.
22) Genes are chemical instructions. Give details of exactly what instructions they give.
23) How many pairs of chromosomes are there in a normal human cell nucleus?
24) What are X and Y chromosomes to do with? Who has what combination?
25) Copy and complete the genetic inheritance diagram and the checker-board diagram to show how these genes are passed on.

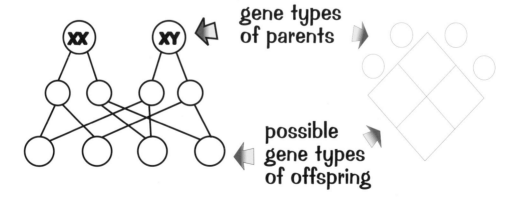

gene types of parents

possible gene types of offspring

26) What are the four main stages of the female menstrual cycle?
27) What are the two main hormones involved in the female menstrual cycle?
28) Give two examples of ways to control the menstrual cycle.

Rates of Reaction

The Rate of a Reaction Depends on Four Things:

1) *TEMPERATURE*
2) *CONCENTRATION* — (or *PRESSURE* for gases)
3) *CATALYST*
4) *SIZE OF PARTICLES* — (or *SURFACE AREA*)

LEARN THEM!

Typical Graphs for Rate of Reaction

The plot below shows how the speed of a particular reaction varies under *different conditions*. The quickest reaction is shown by the line that becomes *flat* in the *least* time. The line that flattens out first must have the *steepest slope* compared to all the others, making it possible to spot the slowest and fastest reactions.

1) *Graph 1* represents the original *fairly slow* reaction. The graph is not too steep.
2) *Graphs 2 and 3* represent the reaction taking place *quicker* but with the *same initial amounts*. The slope of the graphs gets steeper
3) The *increased rate* could be due to *any* of these:

   a) increase in *temperature*
   b) increase in *concentration* (or pressure)
   c) *catalyst* added
   d) solid reactant crushed up into *smaller bits*.

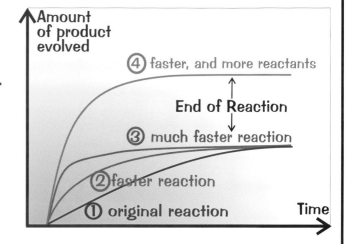

Amount of product evolved

④ faster, and more reactants

End of Reaction

③ much faster reaction

② faster reaction

① original reaction

Time

4) *Graph 4* produces *more product* as well as going *faster*. This can *only* happen if *more reactant(s)* are added at the start. *Graphs 1, 2, and 3* all converge at the same level, showing that they all produce the same amount of product, although they take *different* times to get there.

Reactions can go at all sorts of different rates

1) One of the *slowest* is the *rusting* of iron (it's not slow enough though — what about my little MGB).
2) A *moderate speed* reaction is a *metal* (like magnesium) reacting with *acid* to produce a gentle stream of *bubbles*.
3) A *really fast* reaction is an *explosion*, where it's all over in a *fraction* of a second.

Revision of reaction rates — goes down like a bomb...

Lets face it, chemistry doesn't come much *easier* than this. Or as *exciting* — there's explosions, bubbles and all sorts on this page. Wow. Anyway, only a few points to learn here. Make sure you *learn* the points in the box — and then *learn* the rest of the page as well.

Rates of Reaction

Three ways to Measure the Speed of a Reaction

The _speed of reaction_ can be observed _either_ by how quickly the reactants are used up or how quickly the products are forming. It's usually a lot easier to measure _products forming_. There are _three_ different ways that the speed of a reaction can be _measured_:

1) Precipitation

1) This is when the product of the reaction is a _precipitate_ which _clouds_ the solution.
2) Observe a _marker_ through the solution and measure how long it takes for it to _disappear_.
3) The _quicker_ the marker disappears, the _quicker_ the reaction.
4) This only works for reactions where the initial solution is rather _see-through_.

2) Change in mass (usually gas given off)

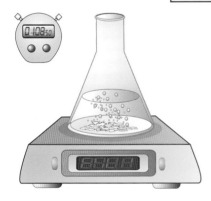

1) Measuring the speed of a reaction that _produces a gas_ can be carried out on a _mass balance_.
2) As the gas is released the mass _disappearing_ is easily measured on the balance.
3) The _quicker_ the reading on the balance _decreases_, the _faster_ the reaction.
4) _Rate of reaction graphs_ are particulary easy to plot from the results from this method.
5) This is the _most accurate_ of the three methods described on this page because the mass balance is very accurate.

3) The volume of gas given off

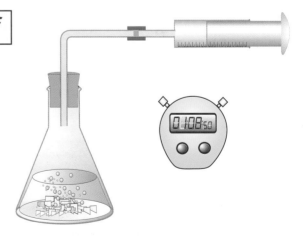

1) This involves the use of a _gas syringe_ to measure the _volume_ of gas given off.
2) The _more_ gas given off during a given _time interval_, the _faster_ the rate of reaction.
3) A graph of _gas volume_ against _time elapsed_ could be plotted to give a rate of reaction graph (see P.24).

How to get a fast, furious reaction — crack a wee joke...

There's all sorts of bits and bobs of information on this page. To learn it all, you've got to learn to split it up into separate sections and do them one at a time. Practise by _covering the page_ and seeing how much you can _scribble down_ for each section. _Then try again, and again..._

Collision Theory

Particles need to collide to react

Reaction rates are explained perfectly by _Collision Theory_.
It's really simple. It just says:

1) The _rate_ of a reaction simply depends on how _often_ and how _hard_ the reacting particles _collide_ with each other.
2) The basic idea is that particles have to _collide_ in order to _react_.
3) They also have to collide _hard enough_.

More Collisions increases the Rate of Reaction

All _four_ methods of increasing the _rate of reactions_ as listed on P.24 can be _explained_ in terms of increasing the _number of collisions_ between the reacting particles:

1) TEMPERATURE increases the Number of Collisions

1) When the _temperature_ is _increased_ the particles all move _quicker_.
2) If they're moving quicker, they're going to have _more collisions_.
3) Even _small_ increases in temperature can have surprisingly _large_ effects on the reaction rate.
4) Since the particles are hitting each other with _greater force_, they are also more likely to react to form new products.
5) An experiment about the effect of _temperature_ on _rate of reaction_ is detailed overleaf.

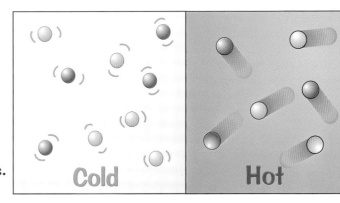

Cold   Hot

2) More CONCENTRATION (or PRESSURE) Means more Collisions

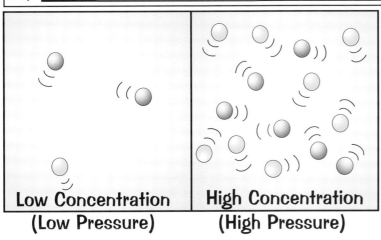

Low Concentration
(Low Pressure)

High Concentration
(High Pressure)

1) If the solution is made more _concentrated_ it means there are more particles of _reactant_ knocking about between the water molecules.
2) This makes collisions between the _important_ particles _more likely_.
3) If the particles are _more likely_ to collide, then they are _more likely_ to react.
4) Hence an _increase_ in concentration causes an _increase_ in reaction rate.

5) In a _gas_, increasing the _pressure_ means the molecules are _more squashed up_ together so there are going to be _more collisions_.

Collision Theory

3) Increasing the SURFACE AREA increases the Collisions

1) If one of the reactants is a _solid_ then _breaking it up_ into _smaller_ pieces will _increase_ its surface area.
2) This means the particles around it in the solution will have _more_ area to work on so there'll be _more_ useful collisions.
3) Remember, more collisions means _quicker_ reactions.

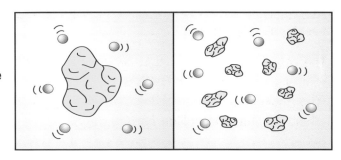

4) A CATALYST increases the Number of Collisions

1) A _catalyst_ works by giving the _reacting particles_ a _surface_ to _stick to_ where they can _bump_ into each other.
2) This obviously increases the _number of collisions_ too.
3) For more on catalysts and how they affect reaction rates, see P.28.

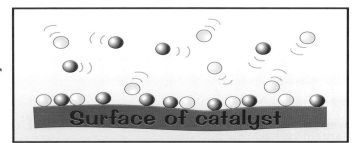

Surface of catalyst

Faster Collisions increase the Rate of Reaction

Higher temperature also increases the _energy_ of the collisions, because it makes all the particles move _faster_. It is _only_ higher temperature (and _not_ surface area, concentration or the presence of a catalyst) that _increases_ the particle's energy — remember that for the Exam.

Faster collisions are ONLY caused by increasing the temperature

1) Reactions _only_ happen if the particles collide with _enough_ energy.
2) At a _higher temperature_ there will be _more particles_ colliding with _enough energy_ to make the reaction happen.
3) This _initial_ energy is known as the _activation energy_, and it's needed to _break_ the initial bonds.
4) Once the activation energy has been reached, the reaction has _enough energy_ to _start_.

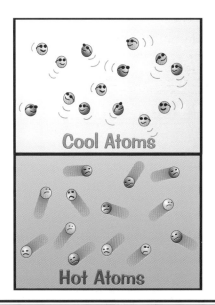

Cool Atoms

Hot Atoms

Collision Theory — I reckon it's always women drivers...

This is quite easy I think. Isn't it all kind of obvious — at least once you've been told it, anyway. The more often particles collide and the harder they hit, the greater the reaction rate. There's a few extra picky details of course (isn't there always!), _but you've only got to LEARN them..._

Catalysts

Many reactions can be *speeded up* by adding a *catalyst*.

1) Catalysts Increase the Speed of the Reaction

A *CATALYST* is a substance which *INCREASES* the speed of a reaction, without being *CHANGED* or *USED UP* in the reaction.

2) Catalysts work best when they have a Big Surface Area

1) Catalysts are usually used as a *powder* or *pellets* or a *fine gauze*.
2) This gives them *maximum surface area* to enable the reacting particles to *meet up* and do the business.

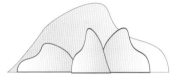

Catalyst Powder

Catalyst Pellets

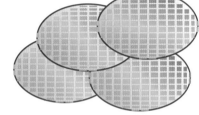

Catalyst Gauzes

3) Catalysts Help Reduce Costs in Industrial Reactions

1) *Catalysts* increase the rate of many *industrial reactions*, which saves a lot of *money* simply because the plant doesn't need to operate for *as long* to produce the *same amount* of stuff.

2) Alternatively, a catalyst will allow the reaction to work at a *much lower temperature* and that can save a lot of money too. Catalysts are therefore *very important* for *commercial reasons*.

3) Catalysts are used *over and over* again. They may need *cleaning* but they don't get *used up*.

4) Different *reactions* use different *catalysts*.

5) *Transition metals* are common catalysts in many *industrial* reactions. *Know these two*:

a) An Iron Catalyst is used in the Haber Process

$$N_{2\,(g)} + 3H_{2\,(g)} \xrightleftharpoons[\text{Iron Catalyst}]{} 2NH_{3\,(g)}$$

(See P. 33)

b) A Platinum Catalyst is used in the production of Nitric Acid

$$\text{Ammonia} + \text{Oxygen} \xrightarrow{\text{Platinum Catalyst}} \text{Nitrogen monoxide} + \text{Water}$$

(See P. 34)

Catalysts are like great jokes — you can use them over and over...

Make sure you *learn the definition* in the top box *word for word*. The fact is they can easily ask you: "What is a catalyst?" (2 Marks). This is much easier to answer if you have a "word for word" definition at the ready. If you don't, you're likely to lose half the marks on it. That's a fact.

Tests and Hazard Symbols

You need to know these *FIVE EASY LAB TESTS*:

1) *Chlorine* bleaches damp litmus paper

(i.e. it *turns it white*).

2) *Oxygen* relights a glowing splint

The standard test for *oxygen* is that *it relights a glowing splint*.

3) *Carbon dioxide* turns limewater milky

Carbon dioxide can be detected by the way it *turns limewater cloudy* when it's bubbled through it.

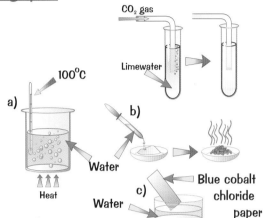

4) *The three lab tests for Water*

Water can be detected in three ways:
a) by its *boiling point of 100°C*
b) by *turning white anhydrous copper sulphate* to *blue hydrated copper sulphate* (and getting hot)
c) by turning *anhydrous cobalt chloride paper* from *blue* to *pink*.

5) *Lab test for Hydrogen — the notorious "Squeaky pop"*

Just bring *a lighted splint* near the gas with air around.
If it's hydrogen it'll make a *'squeaky pop'* as it burns with the oxygen in the air to form H_2O.

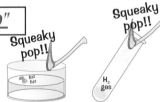

Hazard Symbols

Oxidising
Provides oxygen which allows other materials to *burn more fiercely*.
EXAMPLE: Liquid Oxygen.

Harmful
Similar to toxic but *not quite as dangerous*.
EXAMPLE: Petrol, meths.

Highly Flammable
Catches fire easily.
EXAMPLE: Petrol.

Corrosive
Attacks and destroys living tissues, including eyes and skin.
EXAMPLE: Sulphuric acid.

Toxic
Can cause death either by swallowing, breathing in, or absorption through the skin. *EXAMPLE:* Cyanide.

Irritant
Not corrosive but *can cause reddening or blistering of the skin*.
EXAMPLES: Bleach, children, etc.

Learn the Five Lab Tests — easy as squeaky pop...

This is pretty basic stuff, but people still lose marks in the Exam because they don't make sure to learn all the little details really thoroughly. That's true for just about everything in this book. It's no good just letting your eyes drift lazily across the page and thinking "Oh yeah, I know all that stuff". You've gotta really make sure you *do* know it all. *And there's only one way to do that* — so do it now.

Biological Catalysts

Enzymes are Biological Catalysts

1) _Living things_ have thousands of different chemical processes going on inside them.
2) The _quicker_ these happen the _better_, and raising the _temperature_ of the body is an important way to _speed them up_.
3) However, there's a _limit_ to how far you can _raise_ the temperature before _cells_ start getting _damaged_, so living things also produce _enzymes_ which act as _catalysts_ to _speed up_ all these chemical reactions without the need for _high temperatures_.

Enzymes are produced by Living Things and are Great

1) Every _different_ biological process has its _own enzyme_ designed especially for it.
2) Enzymes have _two main advantages_ over traditional _non-organic_ catalysts:
   a) They're _not scarce_ like many metal catalysts e.g. platinum.
   b) They _work best_ at low temperatures, which keeps costs down.

EXAMPLES: _"biological" washing powders_ and _dishwasher_ powders.

Enzymes Like it Warm but Not Too Hot

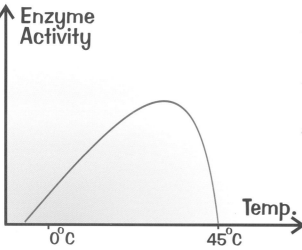

1) The _chemical reactions_ in _living cells_ are _quite fast_ in conditions that are _warm_ rather than _hot_.

2) This is because the cells use _enzyme_ catalysts, which are _protein molecules_.

3) Enzymes are usually _damaged_ by temperatures above about _45°C_, and as the graph shows, their activity drops off _sharply_ when the temperature gets _a little too high_.

Freezing food stops the Enzyme Activity (and the Bacteria)

1) At _lower_ temperatures, enzyme activity also _drops_ quite quickly.
2) This is the idea behind _refrigeration_, where foods are kept at about _4°C_ to keep _enzyme_ and _bacterial_ activity _to a minimum_ so that food stays _fresher_ for _longer_.
3) _Freezers_ store food at about _-20°C_ and at this temperature bacteria and enzymes _don't function_ at all.
4) However, they're not destroyed by _freezing_ and once the food _thaws out_ they spring back into action. So frozen food should be _thawed carefully_ and then _cooked again_ before eating.
5) Cooking _destroys_ all bacteria and enzymes, so _properly cooked_ food is _safe to eat_.
6) However, even _cooked_ foods will go off _pretty rapidly_ if left in a _warm_ place.

"Enzymes" — sounds like a brand of throat lozenge...

This page is definitely a candidate for the mini-essay method. Two mini-essays in fact.
What else is there to say? _Scribble down the facts, then look back and see what you missed._

Uses of Enzymes

Living cells use chemical reactions to produce _new materials_. Many of these reactions provide products which are _useful_ to us. Here are _three_ important examples:

Yeast _in Brewing of Beer and Wine:_ _Fermentation_

1) _Yeast cells_ convert _sugar_ into _carbon dioxide_ and _alcohol_.
2) They do this using the enzyme _ZYMASE_.
3) The main thing is to keep the _temperature_ just right.
4) If it's _too cold_ the enzyme won't work very _quickly_.
5) If it's _too hot_ it will _destroy_ the enzyme.
6) This biological process is called _fermentation_ and is used for making alcoholic drinks like _beer and wine_.

FERMENTATION is the process of _yeast_ converting _sugar_ into _carbon dioxide_ and _alcohol_.

$$\text{Glucose} \xrightarrow{\text{Zymase}} \text{Carbon dioxide} + \text{Ethanol} \quad (+ \text{ Energy})$$

Yeast _in Bread-making:_ _Fermentation again_

1) The reaction in _bread-making_ is _exactly the same_ as that in _brewing_.
2) Yeast cells use the enzyme _zymase_ to break down sugar and this gives them _energy_.
3) It also releases carbon dioxide gas and alcohol as waste products.
4) The _carbon dioxide gas_ is produced _throughout_ the bread mixture and forms in _bubbles_ everywhere.
5) This makes the bread _rise_ and gives it its familiar texture. The small amount of alcohol also gives the bread some extra flavour, no doubt.
6) When the bread is put in the oven the yeast is _killed_ and the _reaction stops_.

Yoghurt _making — only pasteurised milk_

1) _Pasteurised milk_ _MUST_ be used for making _yoghurt_, because _fresh_ milk contains many _unwanted bacteria_ which would give them a _bad taste_.
2) Instead the pasteurised milk is mixed with _specially grown cultures_ of bacteria.
3) This mixture is kept at the _ideal temperature_ for the bacteria and their enzymes to work.
4) For _yoghurt_ this is _pretty warm_ at about _45°C_.
5) The _yoghurt-making bacteria_ convert _lactose_, (the natural sugar found in milk), into _lactic acid_. This gives yoghurts their slightly _bitter_ taste.

With a face like that you could be Chief Curdler in a yoghurt factory, you could pal.

This page is just so easy— it's a blummin' picnic...

This is rapidly turning into a Domestic Science book. Anyway, you're expected to know all these details of making bread, wine, cheese and yoghurt. _Mini-essays again, I'd say._ Enjoy.

Energy Transfer in Reactions

Whenever chemical reactions occur _energy_ is usually _transferred_ to or from the _surroundings_.

In an Exothermic Reaction, Heat is GIVEN OUT

An _EXOTHERMIC REACTION_ is one which _GIVES OUT ENERGY_ to the surroundings, usually in the form of _HEAT_ and usually shown by a _RISE IN TEMPERATURE_

1) Burning Fuels

The best example of an _exothermic_ reaction is _burning fuels_. This obviously gives out a lot of heat — it's very exothermic.

2) Neutralisation reactions

Neutralisation reactions (acid + alkali) are also exothermic.

3) Crystal formation

Addition of water to anhydrous _copper(II) sulphate_ to turn it into blue crystals _produces heat_, so it must be _exothermic_.

ACID

Steam

Don't do it like this!!

ALKALI

In an Endothermic Reaction, Heat is TAKEN IN

An _ENDOTHERMIC REACTION_ is one which _TAKES IN ENERGY_ from the surroundings, usually in the form of _HEAT_ and usually shown by a _FALL IN TEMPERATURE_

Endothermic reactions are _less common_ and less easy to spot.
So _LEARN_ these three examples, in case they ask for one:

1) Photosynthesis is endothermic

— it _takes in energy_ from the sun.

2) Dissolving certain salts in water

3) Thermal decomposition

Heat must be supplied to cause the compound to _decompose_. The best example is converting _calcium carbonate_ into _quicklime_.

$$CaCO_3 \rightarrow CaO + CO_2$$

A lot of heat energy is needed to make this happen. In fact the calcium carbonate has to be _heated in a kiln_ and kept at about _800°C_. It takes almost _30,000kJ_ of heat to make _10kg_ of calcium carbonate decompose.
That's pretty endothermic I'd say, wouldn't you.

Energy

Salt cubes

Food

Take a leaf out of my book — get learning...

An easy page to get you started on energy transfers. It's pretty much common sense really — some reactions like to _give energy out_ (usually in the form of heat) and some like to _take energy in_. Just because you're used to reactions that give _out_ heat doesn't mean they're all like that. Anyway, enough of this waffle. Know what you need to do now? Yip, you guessed it, _get learning_. _NOW_.

The Haber Process

This is an _important industrial process_. It produces _ammonia_ which is needed for making _fertilisers_.

Nitrogen and Hydrogen are needed to make Ammonia

1) The _nitrogen_ is obtained easily from the _AIR_, which is _78% nitrogen_ (and 21% oxygen).

2) The _hydrogen_ is obtained from _WATER_ (steam) and _NATURAL GAS_ (methane, CH_4).
   The methane and steam are reacted _together_ like this:

$$CH_{4\,(g)} + H_2O_{(g)} \rightarrow CO_{(g)} + 3H_{2\,(g)}$$

3) Hydrogen can also be obtained from _crude oil_.

The Haber Process _is a_ Reversible Reaction:

$$N_{2\,(g)} + 3H_{2\,(g)} \rightleftharpoons 2NH_{3\,(g)} \quad (+\text{ heat})$$

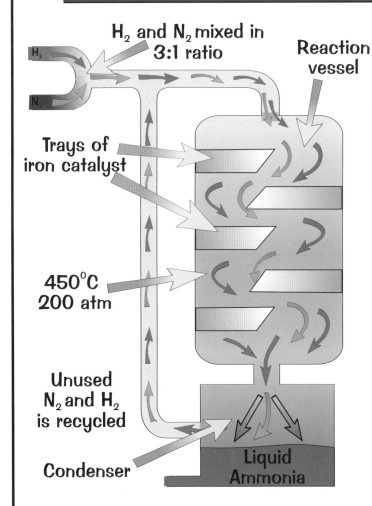

H$_2$ and N$_2$ mixed in 3:1 ratio

Reaction vessel

Trays of iron catalyst

450°C
200 atm

Unused N$_2$ and H$_2$ is recycled

Condenser

Liquid Ammonia

Industrial conditions:

PRESSURE:	200 atmospheres
TEMPERATURE:	450°C
CATALYST:	Iron

EXTRA NOTES:

1) The hydrogen and nitrogen are mixed together in a _3:1 ratio_.

2) Because the reaction is reversible, not all of the nitrogen and hydrogen will convert to ammonia.

3) The _ammonia_ is formed as a _gas_ but as it cools in the condenser it _liquefies_ and is _removed_.

4) The N$_2$ and H$_2$ which didn't react are _recycled_ and passed through again so _none is wasted_.

200 atmospheres? — that could give you a headache..

There are quite a lot of details on this page. They're pretty keen on the Haber process in the Exams so you'd be well advised to learn all this. They could easily ask you on any of these details. Use the same good old method: _Learn it, cover it up, repeat it back to yourself, check, try again..._

Fertiliser from Ammonia

On this page are _two reactions_ involving _ammonia_ that you need to be familiar with. Somehow, I don't think I'd have either of them in my list of "Top Ten Most Riveting Chemistry Topics":

1) Ammonia Can be Oxidised To Form Nitric Acid

There are _two stages_ to this reaction:

a) Ammonia gas reacts with oxygen over a hot platinum catalyst:

$$4NH_{3(g)} + 5O_{2(g)} \rightarrow 4NO_{(g)} + 6H_2O_{(g)}$$

This first stage is very _exothermic_ and produces it's own heat to _keep it going_.
The nitrogen monoxide must be _cooled_ before the next stage, which happens easily:

b) The nitrogen monoxide reacts with water and oxygen...

$$6NO_{(g)} + 3O_{2(g)} + 2H_2O_{(g)} \rightarrow 4HNO_{3(g)} + 2NO_{(g)}$$

...to form nitric acid, HNO_3

Gripping stuff. Anyway, the _nitric acid_ produced is _very useful_ for other chemical processes. One such use is to make _ammonium nitrate_ fertiliser...

2) Ammonia can be neutralised with Nitric Acid...

...to make Ammonium Nitrate fertiliser

This is a straightforward and spectacularly unexciting _neutralisation_ reaction between an _alkali_ (ammonia) and an _acid_. The result is of course a _neutral salt_: (prod me if I fall asleep)

$$NH_{3(g)} + HNO_{3(aq)} \rightarrow NH_4NO_{3(aq)}$$
Ammonia + Nitric acid → Ammonium nitrate

Ammonium nitrate is an especially good fertiliser because it has _nitrogen_ from _two sources_, the ammonia and the nitric acid. Kind of a _double dose_. Plants need nitrogen to make _proteins_.

Excessive Nitrate Fertiliser causes Eutrophication and Health Problems

1) If _nitrate fertilisers_ wash into _streams_ they set off a cycle of _mega-growth_, _mega-death_ and _mega-decay_. Plants and green algae grow out of control, then start to _die off_ because there's too many of them, then _bacteria_ take over, feeding off the dying plants and using up all the _oxygen_ in the water. Then the fish all die because they can't get enough _oxygen_. Lovely. It's called _eutrophication_ (see the Biology Book for more details). It's all good clean fun.

2) If too many _nitrates_ get into drinking water it can cause _health problems_, especially for young _babies_. Nitrates prevent the _blood_ from carrying _oxygen_ properly and children can _turn blue_ and even _die_.

3) To avoid these problems it's important that artificial nitrate fertilisers are applied _carefully_ by all farmers — they must take care not to apply _too much_, and not if it's _going to rain_ soon.

There's nowt wrong wi' just spreadin' muck on it...

Basically, this page is about how ammonia is turned into ammonium nitrate fertiliser. Alas there are some seriously tedious details which they seem to expect you to learn. Don't ask me why. Anyway, _the more you learn, the more you know_. (He said, wisely and meaninglessly.)

Relative Formula Mass

The biggest trouble with *RELATIVE ATOMIC MASS* and *RELATIVE FORMULA MASS* is that they *sound* so bloodcurdling. *"With big scary names like that they must be really, really complicated"* I hear you cry. Nope, wrong. They're dead easy. Take a few deep breaths, and just enjoy, as the mists slowly clear...

Relative Atomic Mass, A_r — *easy peasy*

1) This is just a way of saying how heavy different atoms are compared to each other.
2) The *relative atomic mass* A_r is nothing more than the *mass number* of the element.
3) On the periodic table, the elements all have *two* numbers. The smaller one is the atomic number (how many protons it has).
   But the *bigger one* is the *mass number* (how many protons and neutrons it has) which, kind of obviously, is also the *Relative atomic mass*. Easy peasy, I'd say.

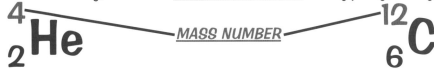

$$^{4}_{2}He \quad \text{———MASS NUMBER———} \quad ^{12}_{6}C$$

Helium has $A_r = 4$. Carbon has $A_r = 12$. (So carbon atoms are *3 times heavier* than helium atoms)

Relative Formula Mass, M_r — *also easy peasy*

If you have a compound like $MgCl_2$ then it has a *RELATIVE FORMULA MASS*, M_r, which is just all the relative atomic masses *added together*.
For $MgCl_2$ it would be:

$$MgCl_2$$

So the M_r for $MgCl_2$ is simply **95**

$$24 \quad + \quad (35.5 \times 2) \quad = \quad 95$$

You can easily get the A_r for any element from the *Periodic Table* (see inside front cover), but in a lot of questions they give you them anyway. And that's all it is. A big fancy name like *Relative Formula Mass* and all it means is *"add up all the mass numbers"*. What a swizz, eh? You'd have thought it'd be something a bit juicier than that, wouldn't you.

Calculating % Mass *of an Element in a Compound*

This is actually dead easy — so long as you've learnt this formula:

$$\text{PERCENTAGE MASS OF AN ELEMENT IN A COMPOUND} = \frac{A_r \times \text{No. of atoms (of that element)}}{M_r \text{ (of whole compound)}} \times 100$$

If you don't learn the formula then you'd better be pretty smart — or you'll struggle.
EXAMPLE: Find the percentage mass of sodium in sodium carbonate, Na_2CO_3
ANSWER:
   A_r of sodium = 23, A_r of carbon = 12, A_r of oxygen = 16
   M_r of Na_2CO_3 = $(2 \times 23) + 12 + (3 \times 16) = 106$

Now use the formula: $\quad \text{Percentage mass} = \dfrac{A_r \times n}{M_r} \times 100 = \dfrac{23 \times 2}{106} \times 100 = \mathbf{43.4\%}$

And there you have it. Sodium represents *43.4%* of the mass of sodium carbonate.

Phew, Chemistry — scary stuff sometimes, innit...

When you know it, *cover the page* and *scribble down* the important details. D'ya miss any?
1) Use the periodic table to find the relative atomic mass of these elements: Cu, K, Kr, Fe, Cl
2) Find the percentage mass of oxygen in these: a) Fe_2O_3 b) H_2O c) $CaCO_3$ d) H_2SO_4

Revision Summary for Module Seven

This module isn't too bad really. I suppose some of the stuff on Rates of Reaction and Relative Formula Mass gets a bit chewy in places, but the rest is all a bit of a breeze really, isn't it? Anyway, here's some more of those nice easy questions which you enjoy so much. Remember, if you can't answer one, look at the appropriate page and learn it. Then go back and try them again. Your hope is that one day you'll be able to glide effortlessly through all of them — it's a nice trick if you can do it.

1) What are the four factors which the rate of a reaction depends on?
2) Sketch a typical rate of reaction graph. How would the graph differ if:
    a) the concentration was increased
    b) the temperature was increased
    c) the initial amount of reactants was decreased?
3) What are the three different ways of measuring the speed of a reaction? Describe each method as fully as possible, using a diagram.
4) Explain how each of the four factors that increase the rate of a reaction increase the *number of collisions* between particles.
5) What is the other aspect of collision theory which determines the rate of reaction?
6) Which is the only physical factor which affects this other aspect of the collisions?
7) What is the definition of a catalyst?
8) Why is it best to maximise the surface area of a catalyst? How is this done?
9) Name two specific industrial catalysts and give the process they are used in.
10) Describe, using diagrams, the five 'easy' lab tests. What is each one designed to detect?
11) Draw diagrams of the six hazard symbols. Give an example of each hazard.
12) What are enzymes? Where are they made? Give three examples of their use by man.
13) Sketch the graph for enzyme activity vs temperature, indicating the temperatures.
14) What effect does freezing have on food? What happens when you thaw it out?
15) Give the word-equation for fermentation. Which organism and which enzyme are involved?
16) Explain what happens in brewing and bread-making. What is the difference between them?
17) What kind of milk is needed for making cheese and yoghurt and why?
18) What gives yoghurt and cheese their flavour?
19) What are endothermic and exothermic reactions? Give three examples of each type.
20) What is the Haber process? What are the raw materials for it and how are they obtained?
21) Draw a full diagram for the Haber process and explain the temperature and pressure used.
22) Give full details of how ammonia is turned into nitric acid, including equations.
23) What is the main use of ammonia? Give the equation for producing ammonium nitrate.
24) Give two problems resulting from the use of nitrate fertilisers.
25) What are A_r and M_r?
26) What is the relationship between A_r and the number of protons and neutrons in the atom?
27) Find A_r or M_r for these (use the periodic table inside the front cover):
    a) Ca   b) Ag   c) CO_2 d) $MgCO_3$ e) Na_2CO_3 f) ZnO   g) KOH   h) NH_3
    i) butane   j) sodium chloride
28) What is the formula for calculating the percentage mass of an element in a compound?
    a) Calculate the percentage mass of oxygen in magnesium oxide, MgO
    b) Calculate the percentage mass of carbon in   i) $CaCO_3$ ii) CO_2 iii) Methane
    c) Calculate the percentage mass of metal in these oxides: i) Na_2O ii) Fe_2O_3 iii) Al_2O_3

Solids, Liquids and Gases

These are known as the _three states of matter_. Make sure you know everything there is to know.

Solids _have_ Strong Forces of Attraction

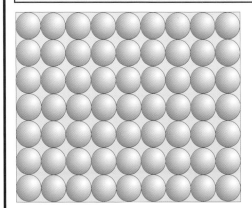

1) There are _strong forces_ of _attraction_ between molecules.
2) The molecules are held in _fixed positions_ in a very regular lattice arrangement.
3) They _don't_ move from their positions, so all solids keep a definite _shape_ and _volume_, and don't flow like liquids.
4) They _vibrate_ about their positions.
   The _hotter_ the solid becomes, the _more_ they _vibrate_.
   This causes solids to _expand_ slightly when heated.
5) Solids _can't be compressed_ because the molecules are already packed _very_ closely together.
6) Solids are generally _very_ dense.

Liquids _have_ Moderate Forces of Attraction

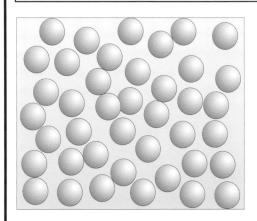

1) There is _some_ force of _attraction_ between the molecules.
2) The molecules are _free_ to move past each other, but they do tend to _stick_ together.
3) Liquids _don't_ keep a _definite shape_ and will flow to fill the bottom of a container. But they do keep the _same_ volume.
4) The molecules are _constantly_ moving in _random_ motion.
   The _hotter_ the liquid becomes, the _faster_ they move.
   This causes liquids to _expand_ slightly when heated.
5) Liquids _can't_ be compressed because the molecules are already packed _closely_ together.
6) Liquids are _quite dense_, but not as dense as solids.

Gases _have_ No Forces of Attraction

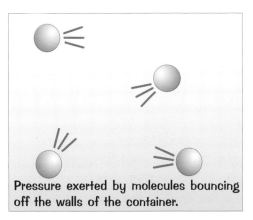

Pressure exerted by molecules bouncing off the walls of the container.

1) There is _no_ force of _attraction_ between the molecules.
2) The molecules are free to move. They travel in _straight lines_ and only interact with each other when they _collide_.
3) Gases _don't_ keep a _definite_ shape or volume and will always _expand_ to fill any container. Gases exert a _pressure_ on the walls of the container.
4) The molecules are _constantly_ moving in _random_ motion.
   The _hotter_ the gas becomes, the _faster_ they move. When _heated_, a gas will either _expand_ or its _pressure_ will _increase_.
5) _Gases_ can be _compressed_ easily because there's a lot of _free space_ between the molecules.
6) Gases all have very low _densities_.

Don't get yourself in a state about this lot, just learn it...

This is pretty basic stuff, but people still lose marks in the Exam because they don't make sure to learn all the little details really thoroughly. And there's only one way to do that: _COVER THE PAGE UP AND SCRIBBLE IT ALL DOWN FROM MEMORY_. That soon shows what you really know — and that's what you've got to do for every page. Do it now for this one, _AND KEEP TRYING UNTIL YOU CAN_.

Changes of State

CHANGES OF STATE always involve *HEAT ENERGY* going either *IN* or *OUT*.

Melting — the rigid lattice breaks down

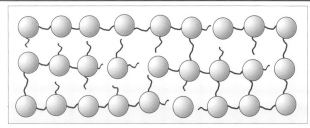

1) When a *SOLID* is *heated*, the heat energy goes to the *molecules*.
2) It makes them vibrate *more and more*.
3) Eventually the *strong forces* between the molecules (that hold them in the rigid lattice) are *overcome*, and the molecules start to move around.   The solid has now *MELTED*.

Evaporation — the fastest molecules escape

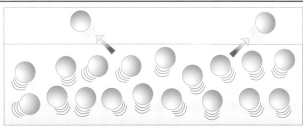

1) When a *LIQUID* is *heated*, the heat energy goes to the *molecules*, which makes them *move faster*.
2) Some molecules move faster than others.
3) Fast-moving molecules at the *surface* will *overcome* the forces of *attraction* from the other molecules and *escape*. This is *EVAPORATION*.

Boiling — all molecules are fast enough to escape

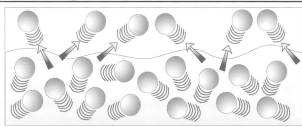

1) When the liquid gets *hot enough*, virtually *all* the molecules have enough *speed and energy* to overcome the forces and *escape* each other.
2) At this point big *bubbles* of *gas* form inside the liquid as the molecules break away from each other. This is *BOILING*.

Heating and Cooling Graphs Have Important Flat Spots

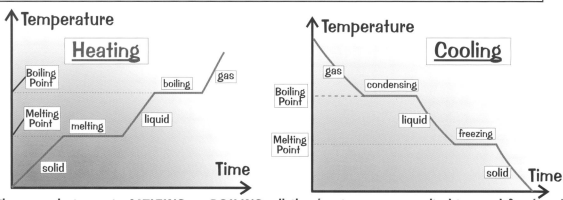

1) When a substance is *MELTING* or *BOILING*, all the *heat energy* supplied is used for *breaking bonds* rather than raising the temperature, hence the flat spots in the heating graph.
2) When a liquid is *cooled*, the graph for temperature will show a flat spot at the *freezing* point.
3) As the molecules *fuse* into a solid, *HEAT IS GIVEN OUT* as the bonds form, so the temperature *won't* go down until *all* the substance has turned to *solid*.

Revision — don't get all steamed up about it...

There are five diagrams and a total of 11 numbered points on this page. They wouldn't be there if you didn't need to learn them. *So learn them.* Then cover the page and scribble them all down. You have to realise this is the only way to really learn stuff properly. *And learn it you must.*

Brownian Motion and Diffusion

1) Brownian motion is the _jerky movement_ of _smoke_ particles, as seen through a microscope.
2) It's caused by _air_ molecules _bumping_ into the _smoke_ particles and knocking them about.
3) The smoke particles _reflect the light_ shone onto them — they're seen as _bright specks_.
4) Brownian motion can also be seen in _pollen grains in water_, looked at through a microscope.

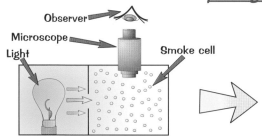
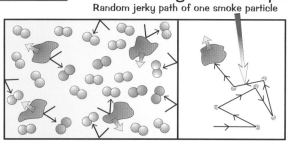

Random jerky path of one smoke particle

Three Gripping Diffusion Experiments

1) _DIFFUSION_ is when two gases or liquids merge together to form a mixture.
2) It happens because the _molecules_ in liquids and gases are in _constant rapid random motion_.
   Make sure you can explain what's happening in these three demonstrations.

1) Purple Potassium Manganate(VII) in water

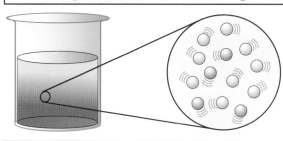

1) As it _dissolves_ into the water, the molecules of the purple potassium manganate(VII) gradually _diffuse_ through the _liquid_.
2) The constant _rapid random motion_ of all the molecules causes the purple colour to eventually spread _evenly_ through the whole liquid.

2) Good old Boring Brown Bromine in Air and in Vacuum

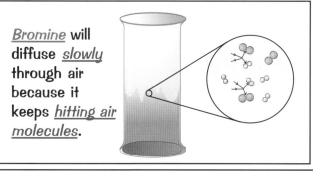

Bromine will diffuse _slowly_ through air because it keeps _hitting air molecules_.

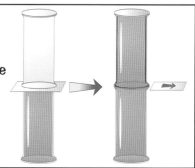

But in a _vacuum_ bromine spreads _instantly_ because there are _no_ air molecules to get in the way.

3) Diffusion of Hydrochloric Acid and Ammonia

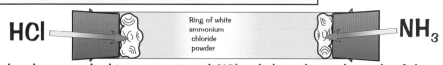

HCl — Ring of white ammonium chloride powder — NH$_3$

1) The cotton wool pads are soaked in _ammonia_ and _HCl_ and shoved into the ends of the tube.
2) The two liquids _evaporate_ and _diffuse_ through the air.
3) When they meet they form _ammonium chloride_, a white solid, visible inside the tube.
4) The _ring of white powder_ forms _nearer_ to the HCl end because the _ammonia_ travels _faster_.
5) This is because ammonia molecules are _lighter_, and lighter molecules always travel _faster_.

Diffusion — it's just a riot, don't you think...

When you think you know the whole page, _cover it up_ and scribble down all the diagrams together with the numbered points for each one. Turn back and _learn_ the bits you forgot. Then try again.

Atoms

The structure of atoms is real simple. I mean, gee, there's nothing to them. Just learn and enjoy.

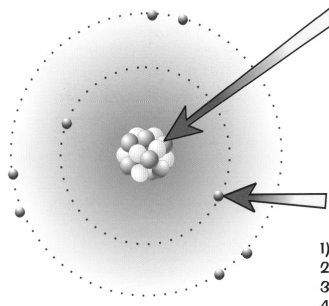

The Nucleus

1) It's in the _middle_ of the atom.
2) It contains _protons_ and _neutrons_.
3) It has a _positive charge_ because of the protons.
4) Almost the _whole_ mass of the atom is _concentrated_ in the nucleus.
5) But size-wise it's _tiny_ compared to the rest of the atom.

The Electrons

1) Move _around_ the nucleus.
2) They're _negatively charged_.
3) They're _tiny_, but they cover _a lot of space_.
4) The _volume_ their orbits occupy determines how big the atom is.
5) They have virtually _no_ mass.
6) They occupy _shells_ around the nucleus.
7) These shells explain _the whole of Chemistry_.

Atoms are _real tiny_, don't forget. They're _too small to see_, even with a microscope.

Number of Protons Equals Number of Electrons

1) Neutral atoms have _no charge_ overall.
2) The _charge_ on the electrons is the _same_ size as the charge on the _protons_ but _opposite_.
3) This means the _number_ of _protons_ always equals the _number_ of _electrons_ in a _neutral atom_.
4) If some electrons are _added or removed_, the atom becomes _charged_ and is then an _ION_.
5) The number of neutrons isn't fixed but is usually just a bit _higher_ than the number of protons.

Know Your Particles

PROTONS are _HEAVY_ and _POSITIVELY CHARGED_
NEUTRONS are _HEAVY_ and _NEUTRAL_
ELECTRONS are _Tiny_ and _NEGATIVELY CHARGED_

PARTICLE	MASS	CHARGE
Proton	1	+1
Neutron	1	0
Electron	$\frac{1}{2000}$	-1

Basic Atom facts — they don't take up much space...

This stuff on atoms should be permanently engraved in the minds of everyone.
I don't understand how people can get through the day without knowing this stuff, really I don't.
LEARN IT NOW, and watch as the Universe unfolds and reveals its timeless mysteries to you...

Proton Number and Mass Number

Come on. These are just _two simple numbers_ for goodness' sake.
It just can't be that difficult to remember what they tell you about an atom.

THE MASS NUMBER ——————— 23

— Total of Protons and Neutrons

THE PROTON NUMBER

— Number of Protons
(sometimes called atomic number)   11

Na

POINTS TO NOTE

1) The _proton number_ (or _atomic number_) tells you how many _protons_ there are (oddly enough).
2) This _also_ tells you how many _electrons_ there are.
3) The _proton number_ is what distinguishes one particular element from another.
4) To get the number of _neutrons_ — just _subtract_ the _proton number_ from the _mass number_.
5) The _mass_ number is always the _biggest_ number. It tells you the relative mass of the atom.
6) The _mass_ number is always roughly _double_ the _proton_ number.
7) Which means there's about the _same_ number of protons as neutrons in any nucleus.

Isotopes are the same except for an extra neutron or two

A favourite trick Exam question: "Explain what is meant by the term _Isotope_"
The trick is that it's impossible to explain what one isotope is. Nice of them that isn't it!
You have to outsmart them and always start your answer _"ISOTOPES ARE..._
LEARN THE DEFINITION:

> _ISOTOPES ARE:_ different atomic forms of the _same element_, which have
> the _SAME_ number of _PROTONS_ but a _DIFFERENT_ number of _NEUTRONS_.

1) The upshot is: isotopes must have the _same_ proton number but _different_ mass numbers.
2) _If_ they had _different_ proton numbers, they'd be _different_ elements altogether.
3) A very popular pair of isotopes are _carbon-12_ and _carbon-14_.

Carbon-12

$^{12}_{6}C$

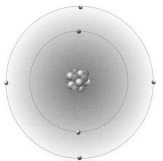

6 PROTONS
6 ELECTRONS
6 NEUTRONS

Carbon-14

$^{14}_{6}C$

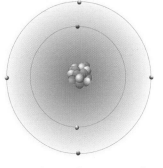

6 PROTONS
6 ELECTRONS
8 NEUTRONS

The _number_ of electrons decides the _chemistry_ of the element. If the _proton number_ is the same (that is,
the _number of protons_ is the same) then the _number of electrons_ must be the same, so the _chemistry_ is
the same. The _different_ number of _neutrons_ in the nucleus _doesn't_ affect the chemical behaviour _at all_.

Learn what those blinking numbers mean...

There really isn't that much information on this page — three definitions, a couple of diagrams
and a dozen or so extra details. All you gotta do is _READ IT, LEARN IT, COVER THE PAGE_ and
SCRIBBLE IT ALL DOWN AGAIN. Smile and enjoy.

Electron Shells

The fact that electrons occupy "shells" around the nucleus is what causes the whole of chemistry. Remember that, and watch how it applies to each bit of it. It's ace.

Electron Shell Rules:

1) Electrons always occupy _SHELLS_ (sometimes called _ENERGY LEVELS_).
2) The _LOWEST_ energy levels are _ALWAYS FILLED FIRST_.
3) Only _a certain number_ of electrons are allowed in each shell:
   1st shell: 2   _2nd Shell:_ 8   _3rd Shell:_ 8
4) Atoms are much _HAPPIER_ when they have _FULL electron shells_.
5) In most atoms the _OUTER SHELL_ is _NOT FULL_ and this makes the atom want to _REACT_.

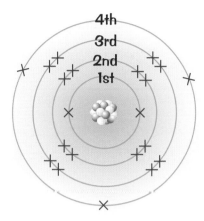

4th shell still filling

Working out Electron Configurations

You need to know the _electron configurations_ for the first _20_ elements. But they're not hard to work out. For a quick example, take Nitrogen. _Follow the steps..._

1) The periodic table (see below) tells us Nitrogen has _seven_ protons... so it must have _seven_ electrons.
2) Follow the '_Electron Shell Rules_' above. The _first_ shell can only take 2 electrons and the _second_ shell can take a _maximum_ of 8 electrons.

3) So the electron configuration for Nitrogen _must_ be _2,5_. Easy peasy.
4) Now _you_ try it for Argon.

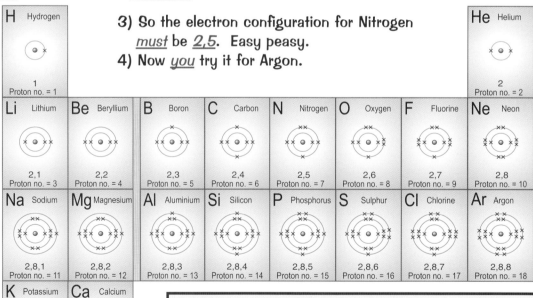

Answer... To calculate the electron configuration of argon, _follow the rules_. It's got 18 protons, so it _must_ have 18 electrons. The first shell must have _2_ electrons, the second shell must have _8_, and so the third shell must have _8_ as well. It's as easy as _2,8,8_.

Electrons rule...

There's some _really important stuff_ on this page and you _really do_ need to _learn all of it_. Once you have, it'll make all of the rest of the stuff in this book an awful lot _easier_. Practise calculating _electron configurations_ and drawing _electron shell_ diagrams.

Elements, Compounds & Mixtures

You'd better be sure you know the _subtle difference_ between these.

Elements consist of one type of atom only

Quite a lot of everyday substances are _elements_:

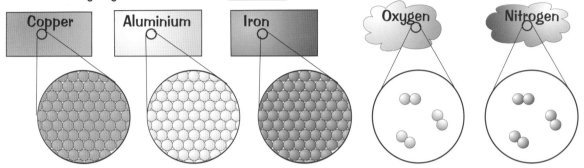

Mixtures _are_ easily separated

1) _Air_ is a _mixture_ of gases.
   The oxygen, nitrogen, argon and carbon dioxide can all be _separated_ out quite _easily_.
2) There is _no chemical bond_ between the different parts of a mixture.
3) The _properties_ of a mixture are just a mixture of the properties of the _separate parts_.
4) A _mixture_ of _iron powder_ and _sulphur powder_ will show the properties of _both iron and sulphur_. It will contain grey magnetic bits of iron and bright yellow bits of sulphur.

Air is a
mixture
of gases

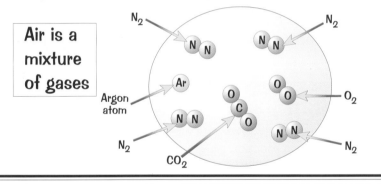

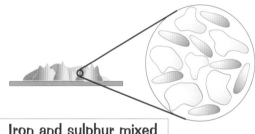

Iron and sulphur mixed
together, but unreacted.

Compounds _are_ chemically bonded

1) Carbon dioxide is a _compound_ formed from a _chemical reaction_ between carbon and oxygen.
2) It's _very difficult_ to _separate_ the two original elements out again.
3) The _properties_ of a compound are _totally different_ from the properties of the _original elements_.
4) If iron and sulphur react to form _iron sulphide_, the compound formed is a _grey solid lump_, and doesn't behave _anything like_ either iron or sulphur.

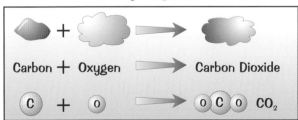

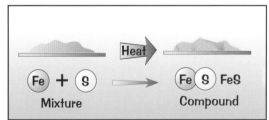

Don't mix these up — it'll only compound your problems...

Elements, mixtures and compounds. To most people they sound like basically the same thing. _Ha!_ Not to GCSE Examiners they don't, pal! You make mighty sure you remember their different names and the differences between them. _Just more easy marks to be won or lost._

Ionic Bonding

Ionic Bonding — Swapping Electrons

In *IONIC BONDING*, atoms *lose or gain electrons* to form *charged particles* (ions) which are then *strongly attracted* to one another, (the attraction of opposite charges, + and –).

A shell with just one electron is well keen to get rid...

All the atoms over at the *left hand side* of the periodic table, such as *sodium, potassium, calcium* etc. have just *one or two electrons* in their outer shell. And basically they're *pretty keen to get shot of them*, because then they'll only have *full shells* left, which is how they *like* it. So given half a chance they do get rid, and that leaves the atom as an *ION* instead. Now ions aren't the kind of things that sit around quietly watching the world go by. They tend to *leap* at the first passing ion with an *opposite charge* and stick to it like glue.

A nearly full shell is well keen to get that extra electron...

On the *other side* of the periodic table, the elements in *Group Six* and *Group Seven*, such as *oxygen* and *chlorine* have outer shells which are *nearly full*. They're obviously pretty keen to *gain* that *extra one or two electrons* to fill the shell up. When they do of course they become *IONS*, you know, not the kind of things to sit around, and before you know it, *POP*, they've latched onto the atom (ion) that gave up the electron a moment earlier. The reaction of sodium and chlorine is a *classic case*:

The *sodium* atom *gives up* its *outer electron* and becomes an Na⁺ ion.

The *chlorine* atom *picks up* the *spare electron* and becomes a Cl⁻ ion.

POP!

Giant Ionic Structures don't melt easily, but when they do...

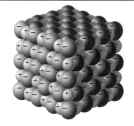

1) *Ionic bonds* always produce *giant ionic structures*.
2) The ions form a *closely packed* regular lattice arrangement.
3) There are *very strong* chemical bonds between *all* the ions.
4) A single crystal of salt is *one giant ionic lattice*, which is why salt crystals tend to be cuboid in shape.

1) They have High melting points and boiling points

Due to the *very strong* chemical bonds between *all the ions* in the giant structure.

2) They Dissolve to form solutions that conduct electricity

When dissolved the ions *separate* and are all *free to move* in the solution, so obviously they'll *carry electric current*.

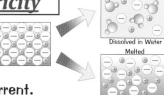

3) They Conduct electricity when molten

When it *melts*, the ions are *free to move* and they'll carry electric current.

Full Shells — it's the name of the game, pal...

Make sure you know exactly *how* and *why* ionic bonds are formed. There's quite a lot of words on this page but only to hammer home *three basic points*: 1) Ionic bonds involve *swapping* electrons 2) Some atoms like to *lose* them, some like to *gain* them 3) Ionic bonds lead to the formation of giant ionic structures. Learn *all* the features of giant ionic structures.

Electron Shells and Ions

Simple Ions — Groups 1 & 2 and 6 & 7

1) Remember, atoms that have _lost_ or _gained_ an electron (or electrons) are _ions_.
2) The elements that most readily form ions are those in Groups 1, 2, 6, and 7.
3) _Group 1 and 2 elements_ are _metals_ and they _lose_ electrons to form _+ve ions_ or _cations_.
4) _Group 6 and 7 elements_ are _non-metals_. They _gain_ electrons to form _–ve ions_ or _anions_.
5) Make sure you know these easy ones:

CATIONS		ANIONS	
Gr I	**Gr II**	**Gr VI**	**Gr VII**
Li^+	Be^{2+}	O^{2-}	F^-
Na^+	Mg^{2+}	Cl^-	
K^+	Ca^{2+}		

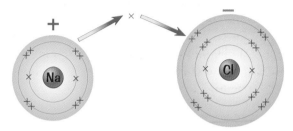

6) When any of the above elements _react together_, they form _ionic bonds_.
7) Only elements at _opposite sides_ of the periodic table will form ionic bonds, e.g. Na and Cl, where one of them becomes a _CATION_ (+ve) and one becomes an _ANION_ (–ve).

> Remember, the + and – charges we talk about, e.g. Na^+ for sodium, just tell you <u>what type of ion the atom WILL FORM</u> in a chemical reaction. In sodium _metal_ there are <u>only neutral sodium atoms, Na</u>. The Na^+ ions <u>will only appear</u> if the sodium metal _reacts_ with something like water or chlorine.

Electronic structure of some simple ions

A useful way of representing ions is by specifying the _ion's name_, followed by its _electron configuration_ and the _charge_ on the ion. For example, the electronic structure of the sodium ion Na^+ can be represented by $[2,8]^+$. That's the electron configuration followed by the charge on the ion. Simple enough. A few _ions_ and the _ionic compounds_ they form are shown below.

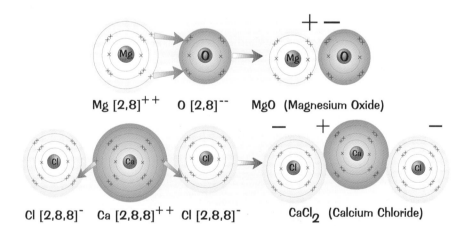

Mg $[2,8]^{++}$ O $[2,8]^{--}$ MgO (Magnesium Oxide)

Cl $[2,8,8]^-$ Ca $[2,8,8]^{++}$ Cl $[2,8,8]^-$ $CaCl_2$ (Calcium Chloride)

Covalent Bonds — Sharing Electrons

1) Sometimes atoms prefer to make _COVALENT BONDS_ by _sharing_ electrons with other atoms.
2) This way _both_ atoms feel that they have a _full outer shell_, and that makes them happy.
3) Each _covalent bond_ provides one _extra_ shared electron for each atom.
4) Each atom involved has to make _enough_ covalent bonds to _fill up_ its outer shell.

Simple ions — looks simple enough to me...

Yet again, more stuff you've _got_ to know. _LEARN_ which atoms form 1+, 1-, 2+ and 2- ions, and why. You need to know how to represent ions _both_ in [x,y] notation _and_ by diagrams. When you think you've got it, _cover the page_ and start scribbling to see what you really know. Then look back, _learn the bits you missed_, and _try again_. And again.

A History of The Periodic Table

The early Chemists were keen to try and find _patterns_ in the elements.
The more elements that were identified, the easier it became to find patterns of course.

In the Early 1800s They Could Only go on Atomic Mass

They had _two_ obvious ways to categorise elements:

| 1) Their _physical_ and _chemical properties_ | 2) Their _Relative Atomic Mass_ |

1) Remember, they had _no idea_ of _atomic structure_ or of protons or electrons, so there was _no_ such thing as _proton number_ to them. (It was only in the 20th Century after protons and electrons were discovered, that it was realised the elements should be arranged in order of _proton number_.)
2) But back then, the only thing they could measure was _Relative Atomic Mass_ and the only obvious way to arrange the known elements was in order of _atomic mass_.
3) When this was done a _periodic pattern_ was noticed in the _properties_ of the elements.

Newlands' Octaves Were The First Good Effort

A chap called _Newlands_ had the first good stab at it in _1863_. He noticed that every _eighth_ element had similar properties and so he listed some of the known elements in rows of seven:

Li	Be	B	C	N	O	F
Na	Mg	Al	Si	P	S	Cl

These sets of eight were called _Newlands' Octaves_ but unfortunately the pattern _broke down_ on the _third row_ with many _transition metals_ like Fe and Cu and Zn messing it up completely.
It was because he left _no_ gaps that his work was _ignored_.
But he was getting _pretty close_, as you can see.

Dmitri Mendeleev Left Gaps and Predicted New Elements

1) In _1869_, _Dmitri Mendeleev_ in Russia, armed with about 50 known elements, arranged them into his Table of Elements with various _gaps_, as shown.
2) Mendeleev ordered the elements in order of _atomic mass_ (like Newlands did).
3) But Mendeleev found he had to leave _gaps_ in order to keep elements with _similar properties_ in the same _vertical groups_ — and he was prepared to leave some very _big_ gaps in the first two rows before the transition metals come in on the _third_ row.

The _gaps_ were the really clever bit because they _predicted_ the properties of so far _undiscovered_ elements.

When they were found and they _fitted_ the pattern it was pretty smashing news for old Dmitri. The old rogue.

Mendeleev's Table of the Elements

H																	
Li	Be											B	C	N	O	F	
Na	Mg											Al	Si	P	S	Cl	
K	Ca	*	Ti	V	Cr	Mn	Fe	Co	Ni	Cu	Zn	*	*	As	Se	Br	
Rb	Sr	Y	Zr	Nb	Mo	*	Ru	Rh	Pd	Ag	Cd	In	Sn	Sb	Te	I	
Cs	Ba	*	*	Ta	W	*	Os	Ir	Pt	Au	Hg	Tl	Pb	Bi			

I Can't see what all the fuss is — it all seems quite elementary...

They're quite into having bits of History in Science now. They like to think you'll gain an appreciation of the role of science in the overall progress of human society. Personally, I'm not that bothered whether you do or not. All I wanna know is: _Have you learnt all the facts yet?_ And if not — _WHY NOT? HUH?_

The Periodic Table

reactive metals | transition elements | poor metals | non metals | noble gases | separates metals from non-metals

The Periodic Table is Ace

1) The modern Periodic Table shows the elements in order of _proton number_.
2) The Periodic Table is laid out so that elements with _similar properties_ form in _columns_.
3) These _vertical columns_ are called _Groups_ and Roman Numerals are often used for them.
4) For example the _Group II_ elements are Be, Mg, Ca, Sr, Ba and Ra.
   They're all _metals_ which form 2+ ions and they have many other similar properties.
5) The _rows_ are called _periods_. Each new period represents another _full shell_ of electrons.

The Elements of a Group Have the Same Outer Electrons

1) The elements in each _Group_ all have the same number of _electrons_ in their _outer shell_.
2) That's why they have _similar properties_. And that's why we arrange them in this way.
3) You absolutely must get that into your head if you want to _understand_ any Chemistry.

   The properties of the elements are decided _entirely_ by how many electrons they have.
   Proton number is therefore very significant because it is equal to how many electrons each atom has.
   But it's the number of electrons in the _outer shell_ which is the really important thing.

Electron Shells are just Totally Brill

The fact that electrons form shells around atoms is the reason for the whole of chemistry.
If they just whizzed round the nucleus any old how and didn't care about shells or any of that stuff there'd be no chemical reactions. No nothing in fact — because nothing would happen.

Without shells there'd be no atoms wanting to gain, lose or share electrons to form full shell arrangements. So they wouldn't be interested in forming ions or covalent bonds. Nothing would bother and nothing would happen. The atoms would just slob about, all day long. Just like teenagers.

But amazingly, they _do_ form shells (if they didn't, we wouldn't even be here to wonder about it), and the electron arrangement of each atom determines the whole of its chemical behaviour.

Phew. I mean electron arrangements explain practically the whole Universe. They're just totally brill.

Electron Shells — where would we be without them...

Make sure you learn the whole periodic table including every name, symbol and number.
No, only kidding! Just _learn_ the numbered points and _scribble_ them down, _mini-essay style_.

Group 0 — The Noble Gases

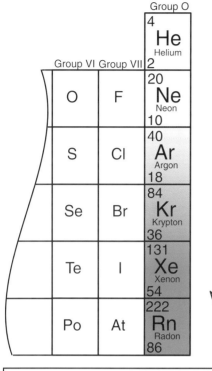

As you go down the Group:

1) The density increases
because the atomic mass increases.

2) The boiling point increases
Helium boils at –269°C (that's cold!)
Xenon boils at –108°C (that's still cold)

They all have full outer shells
— That's why they're so inert

HELIUM, NEON AND ARGON ARE NOBLE GASES
There's also *Krypton*, *Xenon* and *Radon*, which may get asked.
They're also sometimes called the *Inert* gases. Inert means "doesn't react".

THEY'RE ALL COLOURLESS, MONATOMIC GASES
Most gases are made up of *molecules*, but these *only exist* as
individual atoms, because they *won't form bonds* with anything.

Any
noble
gas

Neon   Neon
Fancy a bit   Forget it
of...bonding?   pal!

THE NOBLE GASES DON'T REACT AT ALL
Helium, Neon and Argon don't form *any kind of chemical bonds* with anything.
They *always* exist as separate atoms. They won't even join up in pairs.

Helium is ace!

HELIUM IS USED IN AIRSHIPS AND PARTY BALLOONS
Helium is ideal: it has very *low density* and *won't
set on fire*, (like hydrogen does!)

I love
Helium

And safe too!

NEON IS USED IN ELECTRICAL DISCHARGE TUBES
When a current is passed through neon it gives out a bright light.

ARGON IS USED IN FILAMENT LAMPS (LIGHT BULBS)
It provides an *inert atmosphere* which stops the very hot
filament from *burning away*.

All these
bulbs, argon

Eh? They
look O.K. to me

ALL THREE ARE USED IN LASERS TOO
There's the famous little red *Helium-Neon* laser
and the more powerful *Argon laser*.

He-Ne laser   0 - oh   Argon laser

They don't react — that's Noble De-use to us Chemists...
Well they don't react so there's obviously not much to learn about these. Nevertheless, there's
likely to be several questions on them so *make sure you learn everything on this page*.

Group 1 — The Alkali Metals

Learn These Trends:

As you go _DOWN_ Group 1,
the Alkali Metals become:

1) _Bigger atoms_
...because there's one extra full shell of electrons for each row you go down.

2) _More Reactive_
...because the outer electron is more easily lost, because it's further from the nucleus.

3) _Higher density_
because the atoms have more mass.

4) _Even Softer to cut_

5) _Lower melting point_

6) _Lower boiling point_

Group I	Group II
7 **Li** Lithium 3	Be
23 **Na** Sodium 11	Mg
39 **K** Potassium 19	Ca
85.5 **Rb** Rubidium 37	Sr
133 **Cs** Caesium 55	Ba
223 **Fr** Francium 87	Ra

These _Group II_ metals are quite similar to Group I, except that they have two electrons in the outer shell and form 2+ ions.
They are less reactive.

1) _The Alkali metals are very Reactive_
They have to be _stored in oil_ and handled with _forceps_ (they burn the skin).

2) _They are: Lithium, Sodium, Potassium **and a couple more**_
Know those three names real well. They may also mention Rubidium and Caesium.

3) _The Alkali Metals all have ONE outer electron_
This makes them very _reactive_ and gives them all similar properties.

4) _The Alkali Metals all form 1⁺ ions_
They are _keen to lose_ their one outer electron to from a _1^+ ion_:

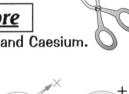

5) _The Alkali metals always form Ionic Compounds_
They are so keen to lose the outer electron there's _no way_ they'd consider _sharing_, so covalent bonding is _out of the question_.

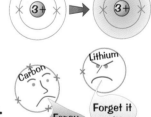

6) _The Alkali metals are soft — they cut with a knife_
Lithium is the hardest, but still easy to cut with a scalpel.
They're _shiny_ when freshly cut, but _soon go dull_ as they react with the air.

7) _The Alkali metals melt and boil easily (for metals)_
Lithium melts at 180°C, Caesium at 29°C. Lithium boils at 1330°C, Caesium at 670°C.

8) _The Alkali metals have low density (they float)_
Lithium, Sodium and Potassium are all _less dense than water_. The others _"float"_ anyway, on H_2.

Learn about Alkali Metals — or get your fingers burnt...
Phew, now we're getting into the seriously dreary facts section. This takes a bit of learning this stuff does, especially those trends in behaviour as you go down the group. _Enjoy_.

Reactions of the Alkali Metals

Periodic Table

Reaction with Cold Water produces Hydrogen Gas

The solution becomes _alkaline_, which changes the colour of the pH indicator to _purple_.

1) When _lithium_, _sodium_ or _potassium_ are put in _water_, they react very _vigorously_.
2) They _move_ around the surface, _fizzing_ furiously.
3) They produce _hydrogen_. Potassium gets hot enough to _ignite_ it.
4) A lighted splint will _indicate_ hydrogen by producing the notorious '_squeaky pop_' as the H_2 ignites.
5) Sodium and potassium _melt_ in the heat of the reaction.
6) They form a _hydroxide_ in solution.
7) This will make universal indicator change from _green_ to _purple_.

$$2Li_{(s)} + 2H_2O_{(l)} \rightarrow 2LiOH_{(aq)} + H_{2(g)}$$
$$2Na_{(s)} + 2H_2O_{(l)} \rightarrow 2NaOH_{(aq)} + H_{2(g)}$$
$$2K_{(s)} + 2H_2O_{(l)} \rightarrow 2KOH_{(aq)} + H_{2(g)}$$

Reaction with Chlorine etc. to produce Neutral Salts

Lithium, _sodium_ and _potassium_ all react _very vigorously_ with _chlorine_ when _heated_. They produce _chloride salts_.

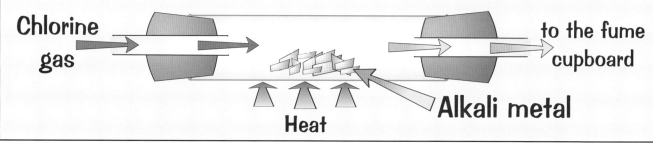

Chlorine gas → → to the fume cupboard

Heat Alkali metal

Learn these easy equations:

$$2Li_{(s)} + Cl_{2(g)} \rightarrow 2LiCl_{(s)} \text{ (lithium chloride)}$$
$$2Na_{(s)} + Cl_{2(g)} \rightarrow 2NaCl_{(s)} \text{ (sodium chloride)}$$
$$2K_{(s)} + Cl_{2(g)} \rightarrow 2KCl_{(s)} \text{ (potassium chloride)}$$

Fluorine, _bromine_ and _iodine_ produce similar salts such as _lithium fluoride_ or _potassium bromide_ or _sodium iodide_ etc. etc. All these _alkali metal salts_ will cheerfully _dissolve_ in water.

Reactions of the Alkali Metals

Alkali Metals burn in Air to produce Oxides

All the alkali metals _burn in air_ and in the process turn into oxides.
You ought to be able to repeat these easy equations with no more effort than a mere flick of the pencil:

$$4Li_{(s)} + O_{2(g)} \rightarrow 2Li_2O_{(s)} \quad \text{(lithium oxide)}$$

$$4Na_{(s)} + O_{2(g)} \rightarrow 2Na_2O_{(s)} \quad \text{(sodium oxide)}$$

$$4K_{(s)} + O_{2(g)} \rightarrow 2K_2O_{(s)} \quad \text{(potassium oxide)}$$

They all _burn in air_ with _pretty coloured flames_:

Lithium burns with a _Bright red_ flame:

Sodium burns with a _Bright orange_ flame:

Potassium burns with a _Bright lilac_ flame:

Alkali Metal Oxides and Hydroxides are Alkaline

This means that they'll react with _acids_ to form _neutral salts_, like this:

$$NaOH + HCl \rightarrow H_2O + NaCl \quad \text{(a salt)}$$
$$Na_2O + 2HCl \rightarrow H_2O + 2NaCl \quad \text{(a salt)}$$
$$KOH + HCl \rightarrow H_2O + KCl \quad \text{(a salt)}$$
$$K_2O + 2HCl \rightarrow H_2O + 2KCl \quad \text{(a salt)}$$

All Alkali Metal Compounds look like "Salt" and Dissolve with Glee

1) All alkali metal compounds are _ionic_, so they form _crystals_ which _dissolve_ easily.

2) They're all very _stable_ because the alkali metals are so _reactive_.

3) And because they always form _ionic_ compounds with _giant ionic structures_, the compounds _all_ look pretty much like the regular "_salt_" you put in your chip butties:

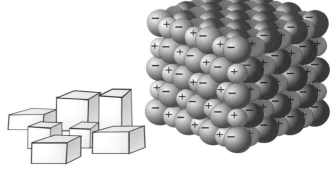

The Notorious Squeaky Pop? — weren't they a Rock Band...

This stuff's pretty grisly isn't it. Still, if you keep covering the page and repeating bits back to yourself, or scribbling bits down, then little by little _it does go in_. Little by little. _Nicely_.

Group VII — The Halogens

Learn These Trends:

As you go *DOWN* Group VII, the *HALOGENS* become:

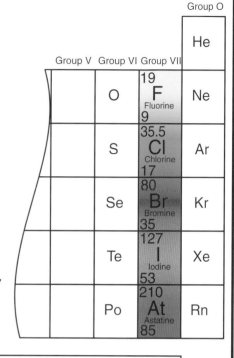

Group O

Group V Group VI Group VII

1) *Bigger atoms*
...because there's one extra full shell of electrons for each row you go down.

2) *Less Reactive*
...because there's less inclination to gain the extra electron to fill the outer shell when it's further out from the nucleus.

3) *Darker in colour*

4) *They go from gas to solid*
Fluorine and *chlorine* are *gases*, *bromine* is a *liquid*, and *iodine* is a *solid*.

5) *Higher melting point*

6) *Higher boiling point*

---

1) *The Halogens are all non-metals with coloured vapours*

Fluorine is a very reactive, poisonous *yellow gas*.
Chlorine is a fairly reactive poisonous *dense green gas*.
Bromine is a dense, poisonous, *red-brown volatile liquid*.
Iodine is a *dark grey* crystalline *solid* or a *purple vapour*.

---

2) *They all form molecules which are pairs of atoms:*

F_2 F F Cl_2 Cl Cl Br_2 Br Br I_2 I I

---

3) *The Halogens do both ionic and covalent bonding*

The Halogens all form *ions with a 1⁻ charge*: F^- Cl^- Br^- I^- as in Na^+Cl^- or $Fe^{3+}Br^-$
They form *covalent bonds* with *themselves* and in various *molecular compounds* like these:[3]

Carbon tetrachloride:

(CCl_4)

Hydrogen chloride:

(HCl)

---

4) *The Halogens are poisonous — always use a fume cupboard*

What else can I say? Use a fume cupboard, or else...

I've never liked Halogens — they give me a bad head...

Well, I think Halogens are just slightly less grim than the Alkali metals. At least they change colour and go from gases to liquid to solid. *Learn the boring facts anyway.*   And smile ☺.

Reactions of The Halogens

1) The Halogens react with metals to form salts

They react with most metals
including _iron_ and _aluminium_, to
form _salts_ (or _'metal halides'_).

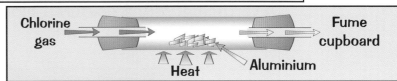

Chlorine gas — Heat — Aluminium — Fume cupboard

Equations:

$$2Al_{(s)} + 3Cl_{2(g)} \rightarrow 2AlCl_{3(s)} \quad \text{(Aluminium chloride)}$$

$$2Fe_{(s)} + 3Br_{2(g)} \rightarrow 2FeBr_{3(s)} \quad \text{(Iron(III) bromide)}$$

Chloride, Bromide and Iodide salts are sorted using Silver Nitrate

Metal halide salts like the ones above are _ionic_ so they usually _dissolve_.
However, the _SILVER_ halide salts are _not_ soluble and this gives a good _test_ for the _three_ halides:

1) Adding _silver nitrate_ to a _chloride_ produces a _white_ precipitate (of _silver chloride_).
2) Adding _silver nitrate_ to a _bromide_ produces a _creamy-coloured_ precipitate (of _silver bromide_).
3) Adding _silver nitrate_ to an _iodide_ produces a _yellow_ precipitate (of _silver iodide_).

2) More reactive Halogens will displace less reactive ones

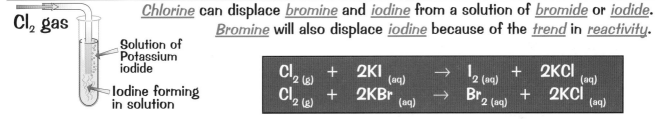

Cl_2 gas

Solution of Potassium iodide

Iodine forming in solution

Chlorine can displace _bromine_ and _iodine_ from a solution of _bromide_ or _iodide_.
Bromine will also displace _iodine_ because of the _trend_ in _reactivity_.

$$Cl_{2(g)} + 2KI_{(aq)} \rightarrow I_{2(aq)} + 2KCl_{(aq)}$$

$$Cl_{2(g)} + 2KBr_{(aq)} \rightarrow Br_{2(aq)} + 2KCl_{(aq)}$$

3) Hydrogen halide gases dissolve to form acids

1) _Hydrogen chloride_ is a _diatomic_ molecule, (a two atom molecule) held together by a _covalent_ bond.
2) It has a _simple molecular_ structure.
3) It is a _dense, colourless gas_ with a choking smell.
5) It _dissolves_ in water, which is very unusual for a covalent substance,
   to form the well-known strong acid, _hydrochloric acid_.
6) The _proper_ method for dissolving hydrogen chloride
   in water is to use an _inverted funnel_ as shown:
7) HCl gas _reacts with water_ to produce H^+ _ions_, which is what

Hydrogen Chloride — Cl H — Covalent bond

Hydrogen Chloride

makes it _acidic_:

$$HCl_{(g)} \xrightarrow{water} H^+_{(aq)} + Cl^-_{(aq)}$$

Hydrogen Bromide and Hydrogen Iodide do the same

Just like hydrogen chloride, these two _gases_ will also _dissolve easily_ to form _strong acids_:

$$HBr_{(g)} \rightarrow H^+_{(aq)} + Br^-_{(aq)}$$

$$HI_{(g)} \rightarrow H^+_{(aq)} + I^-_{(aq)}$$

Salts and Acids — what an unsavoury combination...

More exciting reactions to delight and entertain you through the shove and shuffle of your
otherwise dreary teenage years. Think of all the poor third-world children who never get to
learn about chloride salts and hydrogen bromide — you're very lucky. _Learn and enjoy..._

Transition Metals

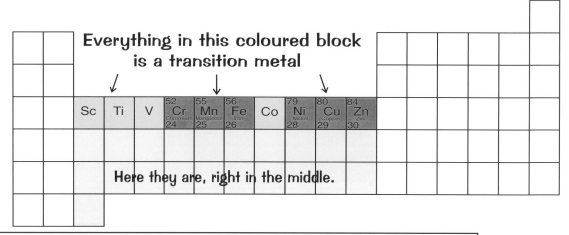

Everything in this coloured block is a transition metal

| | Sc | Ti | V | 52 Cr Chromium 24 | 55 Mn Manganese 25 | 56 Fe Iron 26 | Co | 79 Ni Nickel 28 | 80 Cu Copper 29 | 84 Zn Zinc 30 |

Here they are, right in the middle.

Chromium, Manganese, Iron, Nickel, Copper, Zinc

You need to know the ones shown in red fairly well. If they wanted to be mean in the Exam *(if!)* they could cheerfully mention one of the others like scandium or cobalt or titanium or vanadium. Don't let it hassle you. They'll just be testing how well you can "*apply scientific knowledge to new information*". In other words, just assume these "new" transition metals follow all the properties you've already learnt for the others. That's all it is, but it can really worry some folk.

Transition Metals **all have** high melting point **and** high density

They're *typical* metals. They have the properties you would expect of a proper metal:
1) *Good conductors* of heat and electricity.
2) Very *dense*, *strong* and *shiny*.
3) Iron melts at 1500°C, copper melts at 1100°C and zinc melts at 400°C.

Transition Metals **and their** compounds **all make** good catalysts

1) *Iron* is the catalyst used in the *Haber process* for making *ammonia*.
2) *Manganese (IV) oxide* is a good catalyst for the decomposition of *hydrogen peroxide*.
3) *Nickel* is useful for turning *oils into fats* for making margarine.

The compounds **are very** colourful

1) The compounds are colourful due to the *transition metal ion* which
they contain. e.g. Potassium chromate (VI) is *yellow*.
Potassium manganate(VII) is *purple*.
Copper (II) sulphate is *blue*.
2) The colour of people's *hair* and also the colours in *gemstones* like *blue*
sapphires and *green emeralds* are all due to *transition metals*.

Transition metals **produce many** useful alloys

parp!

1) The transition metals can be easily *mixed* (when molten)
to produce a *new* metal with different properties to the
original metals. The new metal is called an *alloy*.
2) For example, the transition metals *zinc* and *copper*
make the alloy *brass* for trumpets and tubas.

Lots of pretty colours — that's what we like to see...

There's quite a few things to learn about transition metals. First try to remember the three headings. Then learn the details that go under each one. *Keep trying to scribble it all down.*

Industrial Salt

Salt is taken from the sea — and from underneath Cheshire

1) In _hot_ countries they just pour _sea water_ into big flat open _tanks_ and let the _sun_ evaporate the water to leave salt. This is no good in cold countries because there isn't enough sunshine.

2) In _Britain_ (a cold country — as if you need reminding), salt is extracted from _underground deposits_ left _millions_ of years ago when _ancient seas_ evaporated.

3) There are massive deposits of this ROCK SALT in _Cheshire_.

4) The salt is extracted either by _mining_ or else by _pumping water_ into the deposit, _dissolving_ the salt, and then pumping the salt water back to the surface.

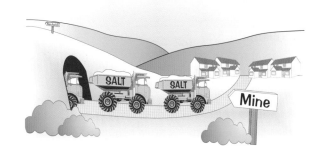

5) Rock salt is a mixture of mainly _sand and salt_. It can be used in its raw state on _roads_, or the salt can be filtered out for more _refined uses_.

1) Salt (sodium chloride) is widely used in the food industry

Salt is added to most _processed foods_ to enhance the _flavour_.
It's now reckoned to be _unhealthy_ to eat too much salt.
So just think about that next time you pour it on your chips.

> _I'm just waiting for the great day of reckoning when finally every single food has been declared either generally unhealthy or else downright dangerous. Perhaps we should all lay bets on what'll be the last food still considered safe to eat. My money's already on Spam Butties._

2) Rock salt is used for de-icing roads

1) The _salt_ in the mixture _melts ice_ by lowering the _freezing point_ of water to around −5°C.

2) The _sand and grit_ in it gives useful _grip_ on ice which hasn't melted.

3) Coincidentally, salt _speeds up_ the _corrosion_ process, making cars rust to bits in no time.

3) Salt is used for making chemicals

Salt is important for the _chemicals industries_, which are mostly based around _Cheshire_ and _Merseyside_ because of all the _rock salt_ there. The first thing they do is _electrolyse_ it.

Rock Salt — think of the pollution as it runs into the sea...

Look at this page. There's all that writing but only about _10 important facts to learn_ in the whole lot. Hmm, I guess that's my fault — too much drivel. Still, if it makes you smile occasionally...

Electrolysis of Salt

Electrolysis of Salt gives Hydrogen, Chlorine and NaOH

Salt dissolved in water is called _BRINE_. When _concentrated brine_ is _electrolysed_ there are _three_ useful products:

a) _Hydrogen gas_ is given off at the cathode.

b) _Chlorine gas_ is given off at the anode.

c) _Sodium hydroxide_ is left in solution.

These are collected, and then used in all sorts of _industries_ to make various products as detailed below.

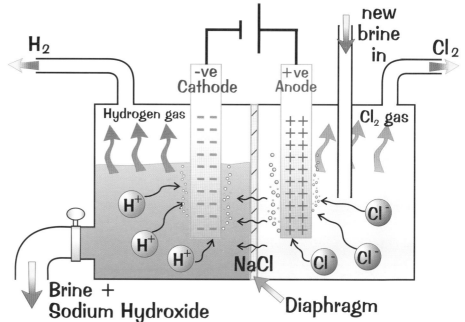

Useful Products from the Electrolysis of Brine

With all that effort and expense going into the electrolysis of brine, there'd better be some pretty useful stuff coming out of it — and so there is... and you have to learn it all too. Ace.

1) Chlorine

1) Used in _disinfectants_ 2) _killing bacteria_ (e.g. in _swimming pools_)
3) _plastics_ 4) _HCl_ 5) _insecticides_. Don't forget the simple lab test for chlorine — it _bleaches_ damp _litmus paper_.

Damp Litmus Paper

2) Hydrogen

1) Used in the _Haber Process_ to make _ammonia_ (remember?).
2) Used to change _oils_ into _fats_ for making _margarine_ ("hydrogenated vegetable oil"). Think about that when you spread it on your toast in the morning. Yum.

3) Sodium hydroxide

Sodium Hydroxide is a very strong _alkali_ and is used _widely_ in the _chemical industry_.
e.g. 1) _soap_ 2) _ceramics_ 3) _organic chemicals_
4) _paper pulp_ 5) _oven cleaner_.

Learn the many uses of salt — just use your brine...

There's even _less_ to learn on this page than on the last one, so you've got no excuse for not _learning it all_. Write down the products from the electrolysis of brine and suggest a few uses for each one. Believe me, you won't get much easier marks in the Exam than these. Giveaway.

Uses of Halogens

Some Uses of Halogens you Really Should Know

Aren't halogens and their compounds ace. *Learn and enjoy.*

Fluorine, (or rather fluoride) reduces dental decay

1) *Fluorides* can be added to drinking water and toothpastes to help prevent *tooth decay*.
2) In its natural state fluorine appears as a *pale yellow gas*.

Chlorine is used in bleach and for sterilising water

1) *Chlorine* dissolved in *sodium hydroxide* solution is called *bleach*.
2) *Chlorine compounds* are also used to *kill germs* in swimming pools and drinking water.
3) It's used to make *insecticides* and in the manufacture of *HCl*.
4) It's also used in the manufacture of the plastic PVC (polyvinyl *chloride*)

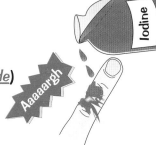

Iodine is used as an antiseptic...

...but it stings like nobody's business and stains the skin brown. Nice.

Silver halides are used on black and white photographic film

1) *Silver* is very *unreactive*. It does form halides but they're very *easily* split up.
2) In fact, ordinary visible *light* has enough energy to do so.
3) *Photographic film* is coated with *colourless silver bromide*.
4) When light hits parts of it, the silver bromide *splits up* into *silver* and *bromine*:

$$2AgBr \rightarrow Br_2 + 2Ag \text{ (silver metal)}$$

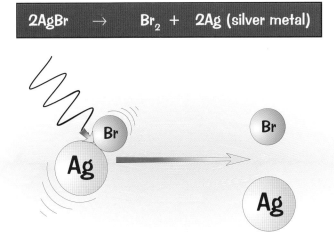

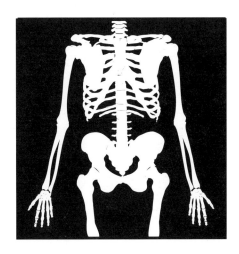

5) The *silver metal* appears *black*. The brighter the light, the *darker* it goes.
6) This produces a black and white *negative*, like an X-ray picture for example.

Well that's pretty much the bare bones of it anyway...

Lots of seriously tedious facts to learn here. And virtually no nonsense. But think about it, the only bit you're gonna really remember forever is that bit about iodine. *Am I right or am I right?*

Chemical Equations

Equations need a lot of *practice* if you're going to get them right. They can get *real tricky* real quickly, unless you *really* know your stuff. Every time you do an equation you need to *practice* getting it *right* rather than skating over it.

Chemical formulae *tell you* how many *atoms there are*

1) Hydrogen chloride has the chemical formula HCl. This means that in any molecule of hydrogen chloride there will be: <u>one</u> atom of hydrogen bonded to <u>one</u> atom of chlorine.

2) Ammonia has the formula NH_3. This means that in any molecule of ammonia there will be: *three* atoms of hydrogen bonded to <u>one</u> atom of nitrogen. Simple.

3) A chemical reaction can be described by the process *reactants* → *products*.
   e.g.   methane *reacts* with oxygen to *produce* carbon dioxide and water
   e.g.   magnesium *reacts* with oxygen to *produce* magnesuim oxide.
   You have to know how to write these reactions in both words and symbols, as shown below:

The Symbol Equation *shows the atoms on both sides:*

Magnesium + Oxygen → Magnesium oxide
$$2Mg \quad + \quad O_2 \quad \rightarrow \quad 2MgO$$

Methane + Oxygen → Water + Carbon Dioxide
$$CH_4 \quad + \quad 2O_2 \quad \rightarrow \quad 2H_2O \quad + \quad CO_2$$

You need to know how to write out any Equation...

You *really* do need to know how to write out chemical equations. In fact you need to know how to write out equations for pretty well all the reactions in this book.
That might sound like an awful lot, but there aren't nearly as many as you think. Have a look.
You also need to know the *formulae* for all the *ionic* and *covalent* compounds in here too. Lovely.

State Symbols *tell you what Physical State it's in*

These are easy enough, *just make sure you know them*, especially aq (aqueous).

(s) — Solid	(l) — Liquid	(g) — Gas	(aq) — Dissloved in water

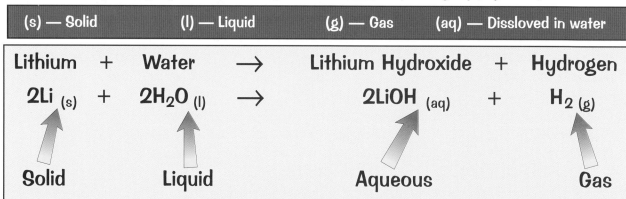

Lithium + Water → Lithium Hydroxide + Hydrogen
$$2Li_{(s)} \quad + \quad 2H_2O_{(l)} \quad \rightarrow \quad 2LiOH_{(aq)} \quad + \quad H_{2(g)}$$

Solid   Liquid   Aqueous   Gas

It's tricky — but don't get yourself in a state over it...

Make sure you know the formulae for <u>all</u> the ionic and covalent compounds you've come across so far. Write symbol equations for the following equations and put the state symbols in too:
1) Iron(III) oxide + hydrogen   →   iron + water
2) Dilute hydrochloric acid + aluminium   →   aluminium chloride + hydrogen (answers on P.90)

Revision Summary for Module Eight

These certainly aren't the easiest questions you're going to come across. That's because they test what you know without giving you any clues. At first you might think they're impossibly difficult. Eventually you'll realise that they simply test whether you've learnt the stuff or not. If you're struggling to answer these then you need to do some serious learning.

1) What are the three states of matter?
2) Describe the bonding and atom spacing in all three states.
3) What are the three ways of changing between the three states of matter?
4) Sketch a heating graph and a cooling graph, with lots of labels.
5) What is Brownian motion? Explain why it happens, and what you'd see.
6) Sketch three gripping diffusion experiments and explain what happens in them.
7) Sketch an atom. Give five details about the nucleus and five details about the electrons.
8) What are the three particles found in an atom? What are their relative masses and charges?
9) How do the number of these particles compare to each other in a neutral atom?
10) What do the mass number and proton number represent?
11) Explain what an isotope is. (!) Give a well-known example.
12) List five facts (or "Rules") about electron shells.
13) Calculate and draw the electron configuration for each of these elements: $^{4}_{2}He$, $^{12}_{6}C$, $^{31}_{15}P$, $^{39}_{19}K$.
14) What is the difference between elements, mixtures and compounds?
15) What is ionic bonding? Which kind of atoms like to do ionic bonding?
16) Why do atoms want to form ionic bonds anyway?
17) What kind of ions are formed by elements in Groups I, II, and those in Groups VI and VII?
18) List the three main properties of ionic compounds.
19) What is covalent bonding? Which kind of atoms tend to do covalent bonding?
20) What two properties did they base the early periodic table on?
21) Who was the old rogue who had the best shot at it and why was his table so clever?
22) What feature of atoms determines the order of the modern Periodic Table?
23) What are the Periods and Groups? Explain their significance in terms of electrons.
24) What is it about the electron arrangements of the noble gases that makes them so unreactive?
25) Give two uses each for helium, neon and argon.
26) Which Group are the alkali metals? What is their outer shell like?
27) List four physical properties, and two chemical properties of the alkali metals.
28) Describe, and write equations for, the reactions of lithium, sodium and potassium with water.
29) What about their reactions with Cl_2? Write equations and draw a diagram of the experimental setup.
30) What compounds are formed when Li, Na and K are burned in air?
31) What about the reactions of the alkali metal oxides with HCl acid? More equations please!
32) Describe the trends in appearance and reactivity of the halogens as you go down the Group.
33) List four properties common to all the halogens.
34) Give details, with equations, of the reaction of the halogens with metals, including silver.
35) Give details, with equations, of the displacement reactions of the halogens.
36) List four properties of transition metals, and two properties of their compounds.
37) Name six transition metals, and give uses for three of them.
38) Where does salt come from? Give two methods of obtaining salt.
39) Describe three large-scale uses of salt, explaining why it is suited to each particular purpose.
40) Draw a *detailed* diagram showing *clearly* how brine is electrolysed.
41) Give uses for the three products obtained from the electrolysis of brine.
42) Flourine and iodine are two of the halogens. What are these two elements commonly used for?
43) Give three rules for balancing equations. Balance these and put the state symbols in:
   a) $O_2 + H_2 \rightarrow H_2O$ b) $Li + H_2O \rightarrow LiOH + H_2$

MODULE EIGHT — STRUCTURES AND BONDING   *NEAB MODULAR SYLLABUS*

Velocity and Acceleration

Speed and Velocity are Both just: HOW FAST YOU'RE GOING

Speed and velocity are both measured in *m/s* (or km/h or mph). They both simply say *how fast* you're going, but there's a *subtle difference* between them which *you need to know*:

> *SPEED* is just *HOW FAST* you're going (e.g. 30mph or 20m/s) with no regard to the direction.
> *VELOCITY* however must *ALSO* have the *DIRECTION* specified, e.g. 30mph *north* or 20m/s, 060°

Seems kinda fussy I know, but they expect you to remember that distinction, so there you go.

Speed, Distance and Time — the Formula:

$$\text{Speed} = \frac{\text{Distance}}{\text{Time}}$$

You really ought to get *pretty slick* with this *very easy formula*.
As usual the *formula triangle* version makes it all a bit of a *breeze*.
You just need to try and think up some interesting word for remembering the *order* of the *letters* in the triangle, s ^{d} t.   Errm... sedit, perhaps... well, you think up your own.

EXAMPLE: A cat skulks 20m in 35s.   Find   a) its speed   b) how long it takes to skulk 75m.
ANSWER: Using the formula triangle: a)   s = d/t = 20/35 = <u>0.57m/s</u>
                                    b)   t = d/s = 75/0.57 = 131s = <u>2mins 11sec</u>

A lot of the time we tend to use the words "speed" and "velocity" interchangeably.
For example to calculate velocity you'd just use the above formula for speed instead.

Acceleration is How Quickly You're Speeding Up

Acceleration is definitely *NOT* the same as *velocity* or *speed*.
    Every time you read or write the word *acceleration*, remind yourself: "*acceleration* is *COMPLETELY DIFFERENT* from *velocity*. Acceleration is how *quickly* the velocity is *changing*."
Velocity is a simple idea. Acceleration is altogether more *subtle*, which is why it's *confusing*.

Acceleration — The Formula:

$$\text{Acceleration} = \frac{\text{Change in Velocity}}{\text{Time Taken}}$$

Well, it's *just another formula*. Just like all the others. Three things in a *formula triangle*.
Mind you, there are *two* tricky things with this one. First there's the "ΔV", which means working out the "*change in velocity*", as shown in the example below, rather than just putting a *simple value* for speed or velocity in.   Secondly there's the *units* of acceleration which are m/s². *Not m/s*, which is *velocity*, but m/s². Got it? No?   Let's try once more: *Not m/s, but m/s².*

EXAMPLE: A skulking cat accelerates from 2m/s to 6m/s in 5.6s.   Find its acceleration.
ANSWER: Using the formula triangle: a = ΔV/t = (6 - 2) / 5.6   =   4 ÷ 5.6 = <u>0.71 m/s²</u>
            All pretty basic stuff I'd say.

Velocity and Acceleration — learn the difference...

It's true — some people don't realise that velocity and acceleration are totally different things.
Hard to believe I know — all part of the great mystery and tragedy of life I suppose.
Anyway. Learn the definitions and the formulae, *cover the page* and *scribble it all down again*.

D-T and V-T Graphs

Make sure you learn all these details real good. Make sure you can *distinguish* between the two, too.

Distance-Time Graphs

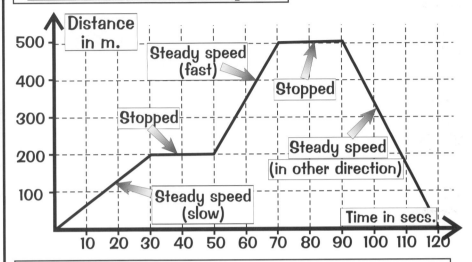

Four Very Important Notes:

1) *Flat sections* are where it's *stopped*.
2) The *steeper* the graph, the *faster* it's going.
3) *Uphill* sections (⁄) mean it's *travelling away* from its starting point.
4) *Downhill* sections (＼) mean it's *coming back* toward its starting point.

Calculating Speed from a Distance-Time Graph

For example the *speed* of the *return section* of the graph is:

$Speed = \dfrac{distance\ travelled}{time\ taken} = \dfrac{500}{30} = 16.7\ m/s$

Velocity-Time Graphs

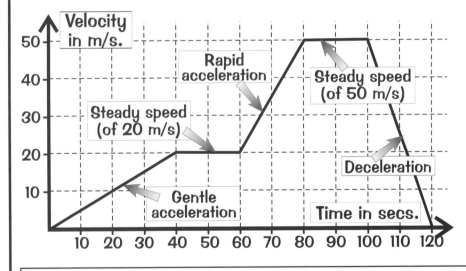

Four Very Important Notes:

1) *Flat sections* represent *steady speed*.
2) The *steeper* the graph, the *greater* the *acceleration* or deceleration.
3) *Uphill* sections (⁄) are *acceleration*.
4) *Downhill* sections (＼) are *deceleration*.

Calculating Acceleration and Speed from a Velocity-time Graph

1) The *ACCELERATION* represented by the *first section* of the graph is:

$Acceleration = \dfrac{change\ in\ speed}{time\ interval} = \dfrac{20}{40} = 0.5\ m/s^2$

2) The *SPEED* at any point is simply found by *reading the value* off the *speed axis*.

Understanding speed and stuff — it can be an uphill struggle...

The tricky thing about these two kinds of graph is that they can look pretty much the same but represent totally different kinds of motion. If you want to be able to do them (in the Exam) then there's no substitute for simply *learning all the numbered points* for both types. Enjoy.

The Three Laws of Motion

Around about the time of the Great Plague in the 1660s, a chap called _Isaac Newton_ worked out _The Three Laws of Motion_. At first they might seem kind of obscure or irrelevant, but to be perfectly blunt, if you can't understand these _three simple laws_ then you'll never fully understand _forces and motion_:

First Law — Balanced Forces mean No Change in Velocity

So long as the forces on an object are all _BALANCED_, then it'll just _STAY STILL_, or else if it's already moving it'll just carry on at the _SAME VELOCITY_ — so long as the forces are all _BALANCED_.

1) When a train or car or bus or anything else is _moving_ at a _constant velocity_ then the _forces_ on it must all be _BALANCED_.

2) Never let yourself entertain the _ridiculous idea_ that things need a constant overall force to _keep_ them moving — NO NO NO NO NO NO!

3) To keep going at a _steady speed_, there must be _ZERO RESULTANT FORCE_ — and don't you forget it.

Second Law — A Resultant Force means Acceleration

If there is an _UNBALANCED FORCE_, then the object will _ACCELERATE_ in that direction.

1) An _unbalanced_ force will always produce _acceleration_ (or deceleration).

2) This _"acceleration"_ can take _FIVE_ different forms:
   Starting, _stopping_, _speeding up_, _slowing down_ and _changing direction_.

3) On a force diagram, the _arrows_ will be _unequal_:

Don't ever say: "If something's moving there must be an overall resultant force acting on it".

Not so. If there's an _overall_ force it will always _accelerate_. You get _steady_ speed from _balanced_ forces. I wonder how many times I need to say that same thing before you remember it?

Three Points Which Should Be Obvious:

1) The bigger the _force_, the _GREATER_ the _acceleration_ or _deceleration_.

2) The bigger the _mass_ the _SMALLER the acceleration_.

3) To get a _big_ mass to accelerate _as fast_ as a _small_ mass it needs a _bigger_ force.
   Just think about pushing _heavy_ trolleys and it should all seem _fairly obvious_, I would hope.

The Three Laws of Motion

The Third Law — Reaction Forces

> If object A **EXERTS A FORCE** on object B then object B exerts **THE EXACT OPPOSITE FORCE** on object A.

1) That means if you _push against a wall_, the wall will _push back_ against you, _just as hard_.
2) And as soon as you _stop_ pushing, _so does the wall_. Kinda clever really.
3) If you think about it, there must be an _opposing force_ when you lean against a wall — otherwise you (and the wall) would _fall over_.

4) If you _pull a cart_, whatever force _you exert_ on the rope, the rope exerts the _exact opposite_ pull on _you_.

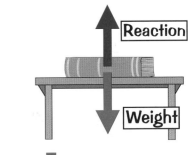

5) If you put a book on a table, the _weight_ of the book acts _downwards_ on the table — and the table exerts an _equal and opposite_ force _upwards_ on the book.

6) If you support a book on your _hand_, the book exerts its _weight_ downwards on you, and you provide an _upwards_ force on the book and it all stays _nicely in balance_.

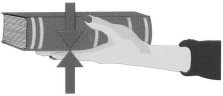

Learn About Those Reaction Force Arrows

In _Exam questions_ they may well _test this_ by getting you to fill in some _extra arrow_ to represent the _reaction force_. Learn this _very important fact_:

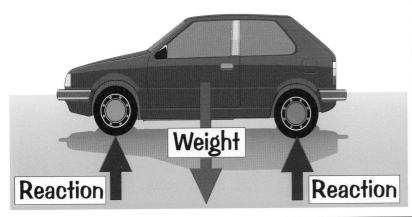

Weight
Reaction   Reaction

Whenever an object is on a horizontal **SURFACE**, there'll always be a **REACTION FORCE** pushing **UPWARDS**, supporting the object. The total **REACTION FORCE** will be **EQUAL AND OPPOSITE** to the weight.

Hey, did you know — an unbalanced force causes ac...

Good old Isaac. Those three laws of motion are pretty inspirational don't you think? No? Oh. Well you could do with learning them anyway, because in this topic there are hardly any nice easy facts that'll help — in the end there's _no substitute_ for fully understanding _The Three Laws_.

Mass, Weight and Gravity

Gravity is the Force of Attraction Between All Masses

Gravity attracts *all masses*, but you only notice it when one of the masses is *really really big*, i.e. a planet. Anything near a planet or star is *attracted* to it *very strongly*. This has *three* important effects:

1) It makes all things *accelerate* towards the *ground* (all with the *same acceleration*, *g*, which = $10 \ m/s^2$ on Earth).

2) It gives everything a *weight*.

3) It keeps *planets*, *moons* and *satellites* in their *orbits*. The orbit is a *balance* between the *forward motion* of the object and the force of gravity pulling it *inwards*.

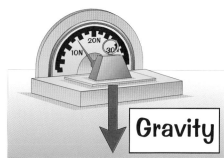

Gravity

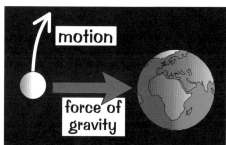

motion

force of gravity

Weight and Mass are Not the Same

To understand this you must *learn all these facts* about *mass and weight*.

1) *MASS* is the *AMOUNT OF MATTER* in an object. For any given object this will have the same value *ANYWHERE* IN THE UNIVERSE.

2) *WEIGHT* is caused by the *pull* of gravity. In most questions the *weight* of an object is just the *force of gravity* pulling it towards the centre of the *Earth*.

3) An object has the *same mass* whether it's on *Earth* or on the *Moon* — but its *weight* will be *different*. A 1 kg mass will *weigh LESS on the Moon* (1.6N) than it does on *Earth* (10N), simply because the *force of gravity* pulling on it is *less*.

4) Weight is a *force* measured in *Newtons*. *MASS* is *NOT* a force. It's measured in *kilograms*.

The Very Important Formula relating Mass, Weight and Gravity

$$W = m \times g$$

(Weight = mass × g)

1) Remember, weight and mass are *NOT the same*. Mass is in *kg*, weight is in *Newtons*.

2) The letter '*g*' represents the *strength* of the gravity and its value is *different* for *different planets*:   *On Earth:*   g = 10 N/kg.
       On the Moon: g is just 1.6 N/kg.   That's because the *gravity is weaker*.

3) This formula is *hideously easy* to use:

EXAMPLE: What is the weight, in Newtons, of a 5kg mass, both on Earth and on the Moon?
Answer: "W = m × g".   On Earth: W = 5 × 10 = *50N*   (The weight of the 5kg mass is 50N)
             On the Moon: W = 5 × 1.6 = *8N*   (The weight of the 5kg mass is 8N)
See what I mean. Hideously easy — as long as you've learnt what all the letters mean.

Learn about gravity NOW — no point in "weighting" around...

Very often, the only way to "*understand*" something is to *learn all the facts about it*. That's certainly true here. "Understanding" the difference between mass and weight is no more than learning all those facts about them. When you've learnt all those facts, you'll understand it.

Force Diagrams

A *force* is simply a *push* or a *pull*. There are only *six* different forces for you to know about:

> 1) *GRAVITY* or *WEIGHT* always acting straight *downwards*.
> 2) *REACTION FORCE* from a *surface*, usually acting *straight upwards*.
> 3) *THRUST* or *PUSH* or *PULL* due to an engine or rocket *speeding something up*.
> 4) *DRAG* or *AIR RESISTANCE* or *FRICTION* which is *slowing the thing down*.
> 5) *LIFT* due to an *aeroplane wing*.
> 6) *TENSION* in a *rope* or *cable*.

And there are basically only *FIVE DIFFERENT FORCE DIAGRAMS* you can get:

1) *Stationary Object — All Forces in Balance*

1) The force of *GRAVITY* (or weight) is acting *downwards*.
2) This causes a *REACTION FORCE* from the surface *pushing* the object *back up*.
3) This is the *only way* it can be in *BALANCE*.
4) *Without* a reaction force, it would accelerate *downwards* due to the pull of gravity.
5) The two *HORIZONTAL* forces must be *equal and opposite* otherwise the object will accelerate *sideways*.

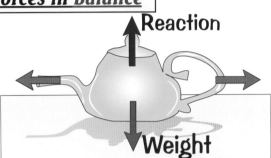

2) *Steady Horizontal Velocity — All Forces in Balance!*

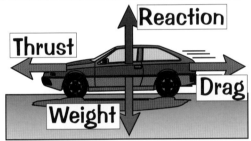

3) *Steady Vertical Velocity — All Forces in Balance!*

TAKE NOTE! To move with a *steady speed* the forces must be in *BALANCE*. If there is an *unbalanced force* then you get *ACCELERATION*, not steady speed. That's *rrrreal important* so don't forget it.

4) *Horizontal Acceleration — Unbalanced Forces*

1) You only get *acceleration* with an overall *resultant* (unbalanced) *force*.
2) The *bigger* this *unbalanced force*, the *greater* the *acceleration*.

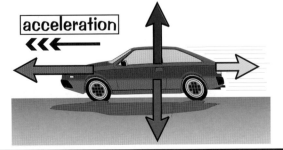

Note that the forces in the *other direction* are still *balanced*.

5) *Vertical Acceleration — Unbalanced Forces*

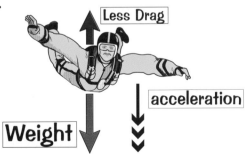

Revise Force Diagrams — but don't become unbalanced...

Make sure you learn those five different force diagrams. You'll almost certainly get one of them in your Exam. All you really need to remember is how the relative sizes of the arrows relate to the type of motion. It's pretty simple so long as you make the effort to *learn it*. So *scribble*...

Friction & Terminal Velocity

1) Friction is Always There to Slow things Down

1) If an object has _no force_ propelling it along it will always _slow down and stop_ because of _friction_.
2) Friction always acts in the _opposite_ direction to movement.
3) To travel at a _steady_ speed, the driving force needs to _balance_ the frictional forces.
4) Friction occurs in _TWO_ main ways:

a) FRICTION _BETWEEN_ SOLID SURFACES _WHICH ARE SLIDING PAST EACH OTHE_

For example between _brake pads and brake discs_. There's just as much force of _friction_ here as between the tyres and the road. In fact in the end, if you brake hard enough the friction here becomes _greater_ than at the tyres, and then the wheel _skids_.

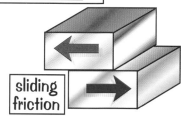

sliding friction

b) RESISTANCE OR "DRAG" FROM FLUIDS (AIR OR LIQUID)

The most important factor _by far_ in _reducing drag_ in fluids is keeping the shape of the object _streamlined_, like fish bodies or boat hulls or bird wings/bodies. The _opposite_ extreme is a _parachute_ which is about as _high drag_ as you can get — which is, of course, _the whole idea_.

2) But We Also Need Friction to Move and to Stop!

It's easy to think of friction as generally a _nuisance_ because we always seem to be working _against it_, but don't forget that _without it_ we wouldn't be able to _walk_ or _run_ or go _sky-diving_ etc. It also holds _nuts and bolts_ together.

3) Friction Causes Wear and Heating

1) Friction acts between _surfaces_ that are _sliding past_ each other. _Machinery_ has lots of surfaces doing that.
2) Friction always produces _heat_ and _wearing_ of the surfaces.
3) _Lubricants_ keep the friction _low_ and thus reduce wear.

Cars and Free-Fallers all Reach a Terminal Velocity

When cars and free-falling objects first _set off_ they have _much more_ force _accelerating_ them than _resistance_ slowing them down. As the _speed_ increases the resistance _builds up_. This gradually _reduces_ the _acceleration_ until eventually the _resistance force_ is _equal_ to the _accelerating force_ and then it won't be able to accelerate any more. It will have reached its maximum speed or _TERMINAL VELOCITY_.

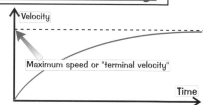

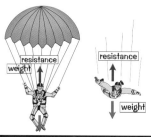

The most important example is the human _skydiver_. Without his parachute open he has quite a _small_ area and a force of "$W=mg$" pulling him down. He reaches a _terminal velocity_ of about _120mph_.
But with the parachute _open_, there's much more _air resistance_ (at any given speed) and still only the same force "$W=mg$" pulling him down.
This means his _terminal velocity_ comes right down to about _15mph_, which is a _safe speed_ to hit the ground at.

Learn about friction — just don't let it wear you down...

I would never have thought there was so much to say about friction. Nevertheless, there it all is, all mentioned in the NEAB syllabus, and all very likely to come up in your Exam. Ignore it at your peril. _Learn_ the six main headings, then the stuff, then _cover the page_ and away you go.

Stopping Distances For Cars

Frictional Forces and Non-uniform Motion

They're pretty keen on this for Exam questions, so make sure you _learn it properly_.

The Many Factors Which Affect Your Total Stopping Distance

The distance it takes to stop a car is divided into the _THINKING DISTANCE_ and the _BRAKING DISTANCE_.

1) Thinking Distance

"The distance the car travels in the split-second between a hazard appearing and the driver applying the brakes".

It's affected by _THREE MAIN FACTORS_:

a) _How FAST you're going_ — obviously. Whatever your reaction time, the _faster_ you're going, the _further_ you'll go.

b) _How DOPEY you are_ — This is affected by _tiredness_, _drugs_, _alcohol_, _old-age_, and a _careless_ blasé attitude.

c) _How BAD the VISIBILITY is_ — lashing rain and oncoming lights, etc. make _hazards_ harder to spot.

> The figures below for typical stopping distances are from the Highway code. It's frightening to see just how far it takes to stop when you're going at 70mph.

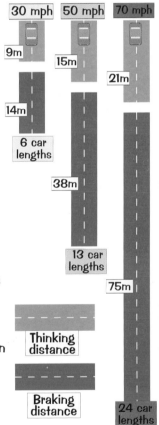

no of car lengths

30 mph   50 mph   70 mph

9m   15m   21m

14m

6 car lengths

38m

13 car lengths

75m

Thinking distance

Braking distance

24 car lengths

2) Braking Distance

"The distance the car travels during its deceleration whilst the brakes are being applied".

It's affected by _FOUR MAIN FACTORS_:

a) _How FAST you're going_ — obviously. The _faster_ you're going the _further_ it takes to stop (see below).

b) _How HEAVILY LOADED the vehicle is_ — with the _same_ brakes, _a heavily-laden_ vehicle takes _longer to stop_. A car won't stop as quick when it's full of people and luggage and towing a caravan.

c) _How good your BRAKES are_ — all brakes must be checked and maintained _regularly_. Worn or faulty brakes will let you down _catastrophically_ just when you need them the _most_, i.e. in an _emergency_.

d) _How good the GRIP is_ — this depends on _THREE THINGS_:
     1) _road surface_, 2) _weather_ conditions, 3) _tyres_.

Leaves and diesel spills and muck on t'road are _serious hazards_ because they're _unexpected_. _Wet_ or _icy roads_ are always much more _slippy_ than dry roads, but often you only discover this when you try to _brake_ hard! Tyres should have a minimum _tread depth_ of _1.6mm_. This is essential for getting rid of the _water_ in wet conditions. Without _tread_, a tyre will simply _ride_ on a _layer of water_ and skid _very easily_. This is called _"aquaplaning"_ and isn't nearly as cool as it sounds.

Muck on t'road, eh — by gum, it's grim up North...

They mention this specifically in the syllabus and are very likely to test you on it since it involves safety. Learn all the details and write yourself a _mini-essay_ to see how much you _really know_.

Work Done and Kinetic Energy

When a _force_ moves an _object_, _ENERGY IS TRANSFERRED_ and _WORK IS DONE_

That statement sounds far more complicated than it needs to. Try this:

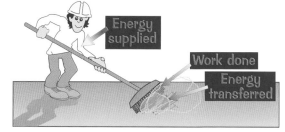

1) Whenever something _moves_, something else is providing some sort of _"effort"_ to move it.
2) The thing putting the _effort_ in needs a _supply_ of energy (like _fuel_ or _food_ or _electricity_ etc.).
3) It then does _"work"_ by _moving_ the object — and one way or another it _transfers_ the energy it receives (as fuel) into _other forms_.
4) Whether this energy is transferred _"usefully"_ (e.g. by _lifting a load_) or is _"wasted"_ (e.g. lost as _friction_), you can still say that _"work is done"_. Just like Batman and Bruce Wayne, _"work done"_ and _"energy transferred"_ are indeed _"one and the same"_. (And they're both in _Joules_)

It's Just Another Trivial Formula:

Work Done = Force × Distance

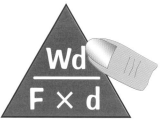

Whether the force is _friction_ or _weight_ or _tension in a rope_, it's always the same.
To find how much _energy_ has been _transferred_ (in Joules), you just multiply the _force in N_ by the _distance moved in m_. Easy as that. I'll show you...

EXAMPLE: Some hooligan kids drag an old tractor tyre 5m over rough ground. They pull with a total force of 340N. Find the energy transferred.
ANSWER: Wd = F×d = 340 × 5 = <u>1700J</u>. Phew — easy peasy isn't it?

Kinetic Energy _is Energy of Movement_

Anything which is _moving_ has _kinetic energy_.

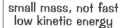

small mass, not fast
low kinetic energy

The _KINETIC ENERGY_ of something depends both on _MASS_ and _SPEED_.

1) The _faster_ it's going, the _bigger_ its kinetic energy (The same car going at a faster speed will have a higher kinetic energy).

small mass, fast
larger kinetic energy

2) The _more_ it weighs, the bigger its kinetic energy (A heavy truck going at the same speed as a light car will have a higher kinetic energy).

big fast lorries Ltd

big mass, real fast
high kinetic energy

Revise work done — what else...

"Energy transferred" and _"work done"_ are the same thing. I wonder how many times I need to say that before you'll remember. Kinetic energy is the "energy of movement". I wonder how many times you've got to see that before you realise you're supposed to _learn it_ as well...

Stretching Springs

Stretching Springs — Extension is Proportional to Load

This is *seriously easy*. It just means:

> If you *STRETCH* something with a *STEADILY INCREASING FORCE*, then the *LENGTH* will *INCREASE STEADILY* too.

The important thing to measure in a stretching experiment is not so much the total length as the *EXTENSION*,

> *EXTENSION* is the *INCREASE IN LENGTH* compared to the original length with *no force applied*.

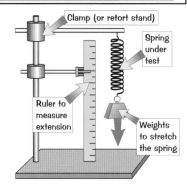

Clamp (or retort stand)

Spring under test

Ruler to measure extension

Weights to stretch the spring

For most materials, you'll find that *THE EXTENSION IS PROPORTIONAL TO THE LOAD*, which just means if you *double* the load, the *extension is doubled too*.

The behaviour of the spring changes at the elastic limit:

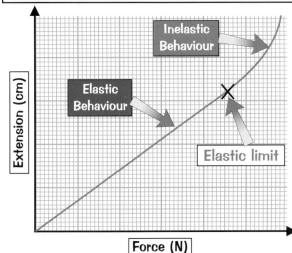

Extension (cm)

Inelastic Behaviour

Elastic Behaviour

Elastic limit

Force (N)

Region 1 — Elastic behaviour

1) In this region when the load is *doubled* the extension *doubles too*.
2) The spring will *always return* to its original *size and shape* when the load is removed.

Region 2 — The Elastic Limit

1) The *elastic limit*. This is the point at which the behaviour of the spring suddenly changes.
2) *Below* this point the spring *keeps* its original *size and shape*.
3) *Above* this point the spring behaves *inelastically*.

Region 3 — Inelastic behaviour

1) In this region the spring *doesn't return* to its original *size and shape* when the load is *removed*.
2) The extension no longer doubles when the load is doubled.

If you put *too much* load on the spring then it will be *permanently damaged*.

You should **LEARN** that this always gives *A STRAIGHT LINE GRAPH THROUGH THE ORIGIN*.

Elastic Potential Energy is Energy Stored in Springs

Elastic potential energy is the energy *stored* when *work is done on an object* to distort it. If a spring is either *compressed or stretched* then it is said to have *elastic potential energy*.

Stretching Springs — always loads of fun...

This is pretty standard stuff, so make sure you know all the little details, including the graph, and the ideas behind the straight bits and curved bits. Also make sure you know about the three regions of the graph. Then find out what you know: *cover, scribble, check, etc.*

Pressure on Surfaces

Pressure is not the same as Force

Too many people get *force* and *pressure* mixed up — but there's a *pretty serious difference* between them.

> **PRESSURE** is defined as the **FORCE ACTING** on **UNIT AREA** of a surface

Now read on, learn, and squirm with pleasure as another great mystery of the Physical Universe is exposed to your numb and weary mind...

Force vs Pressure has a lot to do with Damaging Surfaces

A force concentrated in a *small area* creates a *high pressure* — which means that the thing will *sink* into the surface. But with a *big* area, you get a *low* pressure which means it *doesn't* sink into the surface.

A Force Spread over a Big Area means Low Pressure and No Sinking

Foundations   Snow shoes   Tractor tyres   Drawing pins

 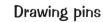

A Force Concentrated on a Small Area means High Pressure and Damage

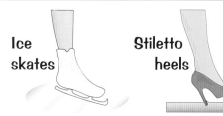

Ice skates   Stiletto heels

Sharp knives

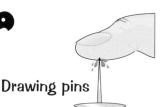

Drawing pins

Pressure in Liquids Acts in All Directions and Increases With Depth

1) In a *gas* or *liquid* the same pressure acts outwards in *all* directions.
This is *different* from solids which transmit forces in *one direction only*.

2) Also, the *pressure* in a liquid or gas *increases* as you go *deeper*.
This is due to the *weight* of all the stuff *above it* pushing down.
Imagine the weight of all the water *directly* over you at a depth of 100m.
All of that is *pushing down* on the water below and *increasing the pressure* down there. This is what *limits* the depth that submarines can go to before the pressure *crushes* the hull or bursts through a weak join somewhere.

3) The *increase* in pressure also depends on the *density* of the fluid.
Air is *not very dense*, so air pressure changes *relatively little* as you go up through the atmosphere. Water *is* pretty dense though, so the pressure increases very quickly as you go *deeper*.

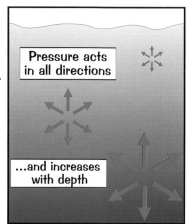

Pressure acts in all directions

...and increases with depth

Spread the load and reduce the pressure — start revising now...

It's funny old stuff is pressure. Force is a nice easy concept and people usually do fine with it. But pressure is just that bit trickier — and that means it can cause people a lot of gip. Make sure you *learn all these details* about pressure. They're all worth marks in the Exam.

Pressure = Force / Area

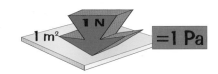 

$$Pressure = \frac{Force}{Area}$$

The normal _unit of pressure_ is the _Pascal_, Pa, which is the same as N/m². There is a fancy definition of the Pascal. If you think it helps, you can learn it:

A pressure of _ONE PASCAL_ is exerted by a _FORCE OF 1N_ acting at right angles to an _AREA of 1m²_

They may well give you questions with areas given in _cm²_. Don't try to _convert cm² to m²_ which is a bit tricky. Instead, just work out the pressure using P = F/A in the normal way, but give the answer as N/cm² rather than N/m² (Pa). Do remember that _N/cm²_ is _not_ the same as Pascals (which are N/m²).

Hydraulics — the Main Application of "P = F/A"

Hydraulic systems all use _two important features_ of _pressure in liquids_. **LEARN THEM**:

1) **PRESSURE IS _TRANSMITTED THROUGHOUT THE LIQUID_**, so that the force can easily be applied _WHEREVER YOU WANT IT_, using flexible pipes.
2) The force can be _MULTIPLIED_ according to the _AREAS_ of the pistons used.

Hydraulic Jack

Car Brakes

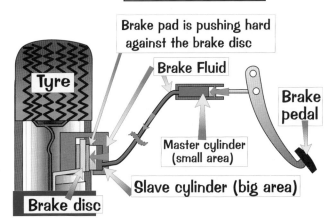

1) All hydraulic systems use a _SMALL master piston_ and a _BIG slave piston_.
2) The _master piston_ is used to apply a _force_ which puts the liquid _under pressure_.
3) This pressure is _transmitted_ throughout _all_ the liquid in the system, and somewhere _at the other end_ it pushes on the _slave piston_ which _exerts a force_ where it's needed.
4) The _slave piston_ always has a _much larger area_ than the _master piston_ so that it exerts a _much greater force_ from the pressure created by the force on the master piston. Clever stuff.
5) In this way, _hydraulic systems_ are used as _force multipliers_. i.e., they use a _small force_ to create a _very big force_ — a nice trick if you can do it.

Learn about hydraulics — and make light work of it...

You certainly need to know that formula for pressure, but that's pretty easy. The really tricky bit which you need to concentrate most on is how that formula is applied (twice) to explain how hydraulic systems turn a small force into a big one. _Keep working at it till you understand it._

The Cause of Days and Seasons

The Rotation of The Earth Causes Day and Night

1) As the Earth slowly _rotates_ any point on the Earth's surface moves from the _bright side_ in the _sunlight_ round into the _darkness_. As the Earth keeps rotating it eventually comes back into the sunshine again.

   This sequence describes _day-dusk-night-dawn_.

2) A _full rotation_ takes _24 hours_ of course — a full day. Next time you watch the _Sun set_, try to _imagine yourself_ helpless on that _big rotating ball_ as you move silently across the _twilight zone_ and into the _shadows_.

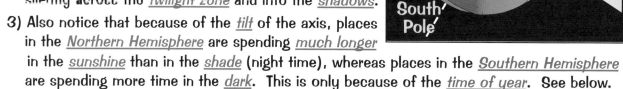

3) Also notice that because of the _tilt_ of the axis, places in the _Northern Hemisphere_ are spending _much longer_ in the _sunshine_ than in the _shade_ (night time), whereas places in the _Southern Hemisphere_ are spending more time in the _dark_. This is only because of the _time of year_. See below.

4) Also notice that the further towards the _Poles_ you get, the _longer_ the days are in _summer_ and the longer the _nights_ are in _winter_. Places inside the _arctic circle_ have _24 hours a day_ of sunlight for a few days in _mid summer_, whilst in _mid winter_ the Sun _never rises_ at all.

5) At the _Equator_ by contrast, the length of day _never varies_ from one season to the next. It's always _12 hours of day_ and _12 hours of night_. The position of the _shadows_ shows all this.

The Orbit of the Earth around the Sun takes 365¼ days

One _full orbit_ of the Earth around the Sun is _approximately 365 days_ (One year). This is split up into _the seasons_:

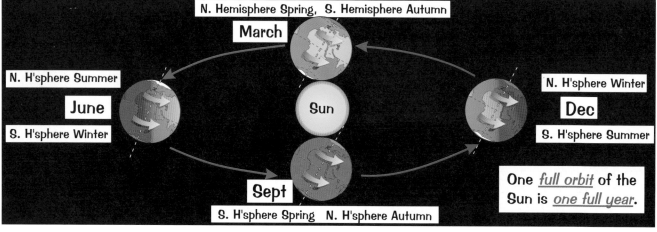

In the dim and distant past _early astronomers_ thought that the Sun and all the planets _orbited the Earth_. i.e. that the Earth was the _centre of the Universe_.

As we all know this was _very wrong_, but then they also thought the Earth was flat, and that the moon was made of cheese.

See Norway at Christmas — take a good torch...

This stuff about what causes the Sun to seem to "rise" and "set" and how the seasons are caused is surely irresistible-just-gotta-know-all-about-it kind of information, isn't it? Surely you must be filled with burning curiosity about it every time the dawn breaks — aren't you?

The Solar System

The _order_ of the planets can be remembered by using the little jollyism below:

Mercury,	Venus,	Earth,	Mars,	(Asteroids),	Jupiter,	Saturn,	Uranus,	Neptune,	Pluto
(My	Very	Energetic	Maiden	Aunt	Just	Swam	Under	North	Pier)

MERCURY, _VENUS_, _EARTH_ and _MARS_ are known as the _INNER PLANETS_.
JUPITER, _SATURN_, _URANUS_, _NEPTUNE_ and _PLUTO_ are much further away and are the _OUTER PLANETS_.

The Planets Don't Give Out Light, They just Reflect The Sun's

1) You can _see_ some of the nearer planets with the _naked eye_ at night, e.g. Mars and Venus.
2) They look just like _stars_, but they are of course _totally different_.
3) Stars are _huge_ and _very far away_ and _give out_ lots of light.
   The planets are _smaller and nearer_ and they just _reflect the sunlight_ falling on them.
4) Planets always _orbit around stars_. In our Solar System the planets orbit the _Sun_ of course.
5) These orbits are all _slightly elliptical_ (elongated circles).
6) All the planets in our Solar System orbit in the _same plane_ except Pluto (as shown).

The Sun is a Star, Giving Out All Types of EM Radiation

1) The Sun, like other stars produces _heat_ from _nuclear fusion reactions_ which turn
   hydrogen into helium. This makes it really hot.
2) It gives out the _full spectrum_ of _electromagnetic radiation_.

Sun

The Relative Sizes of the Planets and Sun

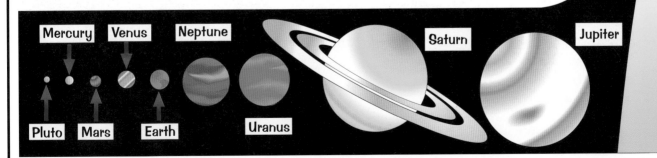

Learn The Planets — they can be quite illuminating...

Isn't the Solar System great! All those pretty coloured planets and all that big black empty space. You can look forward to one or two easy questions on the planets — or you might get two real horrors instead. Be ready, _learn_ all the _nitty gritty details_ till you know it all real good.

Satellites and Planets

Moons, satellites and planets they're all up there if you look hard enough.

Moons *are sometimes called* Natural Satellites.

The planets in our solar system are all _natural satellites_ of the Sun. The planets also have their own natural satellites (moons):

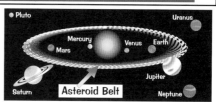

Artificial *Satellites are very useful*

Artificial satellites are sent up by humans for _four main purposes_:

    1) Monitoring _Weather_.
    2) _Communications_, e.g. phone and TV.
    3) _Space research_ such as the Hubble Telescope.
    4) _Spying_ on baddies.

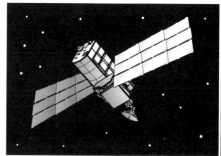

There are _two different orbits_ useful for satellites:

Gravity *Is the Force* which Keeps Everything *in Orbit*

1) _Gravity_ is a force of _attraction_ which acts between _all_ masses.
2) With _very large_ masses like _stars_ and _planets_, the force is _very big_ and acts _a long way out_.
3) The _closer_ you get to a planet, the _stronger_ the _force of attraction_.
4) To _counteract_ this stronger gravity, the planet must move _faster_ and cover its orbit _quicker_.
5) _Comets_ are also held in _orbit_ by gravity, as are _moons_ and _satellites_ and _space stations_.

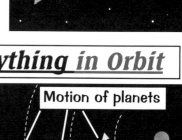

Planets *in the* Night Sky *Seem to* Move *across the* Constellations

1) The stars in the sky form _fixed patterns_ called _constellations_.
2) These all stay _fixed_ in _relation to each other_ and simply "_rotate_" as the Earth spins.
3) The _planets_ look _just like stars_ except that they _wander_ across the constellations over periods of _days or weeks_, often going in the _opposite direction_.
4) Their position and movement depends on where they are _in their orbit_, compared to us.
5) This _peculiar movement_ of the planets made the early astronomers realise that the Earth _wasn't the centre of the Universe_ after all, but was in fact just _the third rock from the Sun_. It's _very strong evidence_ for the _Sun-centred_ model of the Solar System.
6) Alas, the boys at _The Spanish Inquisition_ were less than keen on such heresy, and poor old _Copernicus_ had a pretty hard time of it for a while. In the end though, "_the truth will out_".

Learn This Page — but keep shtum to the boys in the Red Robes...

Planets are ace aren't they. You can see one or two of them in the night sky, just by lifting your eyes to the heavens. Also lots of details about different satellites and the force of gravity to learn. Take in all the other details on the page and then _cover and scribble_.

The Universe

Space, ain't it ace. All those stars, galaxies and solar systems, you could get lost out there.

Stars and Solar Systems form from Clouds of Dust

1) *Stars form* from *clouds of dust* which *spiral in together* due to *gravitational attraction*.

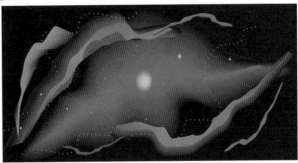

2) The gravity *compresses* the matter so much that *intense heat* develops and sets off *nuclear fusion reactions* and the star then begins *emitting light* and *other radiation*.

3) At the *same time* that the star is forming, *other lumps* may develop in the *spiralling dust clouds* and these eventually gather together and form *planets* which orbit *around the star*.

Our Sun is in The Milky Way Galaxy

1) The *Sun* is one of *many millions* of *stars* which form the *Milky Way galaxy*.

2) The *distance* between neighbouring stars is usually *millions of times greater* than the distance between *planets* in our Solar System. The Milky Way is *100,000 light years* across.

You are here

3) The *nearest star* to us (apart from the Sun of course) is *4.2 light years* away.

4) *Gravity* is of course the *force* which keeps the stars *together* in a *galaxy* and, like most things in the Universe, the galaxies *all rotate*, kinda like a catherine wheel only *much slower*.

5) Our Sun is out towards the *end* of one of the *spiral arms* of the Milky Way galaxy.

The Whole Universe has More Than A Billion Galaxies

You are here

1) *Galaxies* themselves are often *millions of times further apart* than the *stars are* within a galaxy. So that's 4.2 *million* light years apart.

2) So even the slowest amongst you will soon begin to realise that the Universe is *mostly empty space* and is *really really big*. Ever been to the NEC? Yeah? Well, it's even bigger than that.

Galaxies, The Milky Way — it's just like a big chocolate factory...

More gripping facts about the Universe. It's just so big — look at those numbers: 1 light year is *9½ million million km*, one galaxy is *100,000* of those across, and the Universe contains *billions* of galaxies, all *millions* of times further apart than 100,000 light years is. Man, *that's real big*.

Revision Summary for Module Eleven

More jolly questions which I know you're going to really enjoy. There are lots of bits and bobs on forces and the solar system which you definitely need to know. Some bits are certainly quite tricky to understand, but there's also loads of straightforward stuff which just need to be learnt, ready for instant regurgitation in the Exam. You have to practise these questions over and over and over again, until you can answer them all really easily — phew, such jolly fun.

1) What's the difference between speed and velocity? Give an example of each.
2) Write down the formula for working out speed. Find the speed of a partly chewed mouse which hobbles 3.2m in 35s. Find how far he would get in 25 minutes.
3) What's acceleration? Is it the same thing as speed or velocity? What are the units of it?
4) Write down the formula for acceleration.
   What's the acceleration of a soggy pea, flicked from rest to a speed of 14 m/s in 0.4s?
5) Sketch a typical distance-time graph and point out all the important parts of it.
6) Sketch a typical velocity-time graph and point out all the important parts of it.
7) Write down the First Law of Motion. Illustrate with a diagram.
8) Write down the Second Law of Motion. Illustrate with a diagram. What's the formula for it?
9) Write down the Third Law of Motion. Illustrate it with four diagrams.
10) Explain what *reaction force* is and where it pops up. Is it important to know about it?
11) What is gravity? List the three main effects that gravity produces.
12) Explain the difference between mass and weight. What units are they measured in?
13) What's the formula for weight? Illustrate it with a worked example of your own.
14) Sketch each of the five standard force diagrams, showing the forces and the type of motion.
15) List the three types of friction with a sketch to illustrate each one.
16) What 2 effects does friction have on machinery?
17) What is "terminal velocity"? Is it the same thing as maximum speed?
18) What are the two different parts of the overall stopping distance of a car?
19) List the three or four factors which affect each of the two sections of stopping distance.
20) What's the formula for work done? A crazy dog drags a big branch 12m over the next-door neighbour's front lawn, pulling with a force of 535N. How much energy was transferred?
21) What two things affect the kinetic energy of an object?
22) What is the stretching law? Sketch the usual apparatus. Explain what you must measure.
23) Sketch the important graph and explain its shape. Explain "elastic" and "inelastic".
24) What's the definition of pressure? What combination of force and area gives high pressure?
25) Sketch four diagrams showing how pressure is a) reduced and b) increased.
26) What happens to pressure as you go deeper? Which direction does the pressure act in?
27) Write down the two features of pressure in liquids which allow hydraulic systems to work.
28) Sketch a diagram to explain how day and night come about.
29) Sketch a diagram to show how the seasons come about.
30) How long does a full rotation of the Earth take? How long does a full orbit of the Sun take?
31) Which is the biggest planet? Which is the smallest? Sketch the relative sizes of all of them.
32) What is it that keeps the planets in their orbits? What other things are held in orbits?
33) What are constellations? What do planets do in the constellations?
34) List the eleven parts of the Solar System starting with the Sun, and get them in the right order.
35) What do planets look like in the night sky? Which ones can be seen with the naked eye?
36) What's the big difference between planets and stars?
37) How does the Sun produce all its heat? What does the Sun give out?
38) What are natural and artificial satellites? What four purposes do we have for satellites?
39) What do stars and solar systems form from? What force causes it all to happen?
40) What is the Milky Way? Sketch it and show our Sun in relation to it. How big is the Universe?

Waves — Basic Principles

Waves are different from anything else. They have various features which _only waves have_:

Amplitude, Wavelength and Frequency

Too many people get these _wrong_. Take careful note:

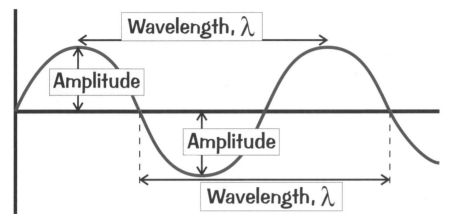

Don't be scared off by the _funny symbol_, "λ", will you.

λ is just a _harmless Greek letter_, called _"lambda"_ (say it as _"lamda"_).
Try it yourself, go on:
    _"L-A-M-D-A"_.
There, you see — doesn't hurt at all, does it.

1) The _AMPLITUDE_ goes from the _middle line_ to the _peak_, NOT from a trough to a peak.
2) The _WAVELENGTH_ covers _a full cycle_ of the wave, e.g. from _peak to peak_, not just from _"two bits that are sort of separated a bit"_.
3) _FREQUENCY_ is how many _complete waves_ there are _per second_ (passing a certain point).

All Waves Carry Energy — Without Transferring Matter

There are lots of _good examples_ which show that all sorts of waves _carry energy_. _Learn these_:
1) _Light_, _infrared_ and _microwaves_ all make things _warm up_. _X-rays_ and _gamma rays_ can cause _ionisation_ and _damage_ to cells, which also shows that they _carry energy_.
2) _Loud sounds_ make things _vibrate or move_. Even the quietest sound moves your _ear drum_.
3) Waves on the sea can _toss big boats around_ and can _generate electricity_.

All Waves can be Reflected and Refracted

They might test whether or not you realise these two things are _properties_ of waves, so _learn them_. The two words are _confusingly similar_ but you _MUST_ learn the _difference_ between them.

1) _REFLECTION_ is when a wave _"bounces off"_ a surface and sets off in a _completely different direction_.
   Reflection of _light_ is obvious, e.g. from any shiny surface like a _mirror_. _Sound also reflects_ — it's called an _echo_. Sound will only be reflected from _hard flat_ surfaces. Things like _carpets_ and _curtains_ act as _absorbing_ surfaces which will _absorb_ sounds rather than reflect them.

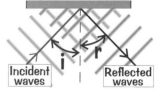

2) _REFRACTION_ is when a wave _changes direction_ as it _enters a different substance_ (or "medium"). All waves refract. Light and sound are _reflected_, _refracted_ and _diffracted_ and this shows they travel as waves.

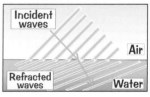

Learn about waves — just get into the vibes, man...

This is all pretty basic stuff on waves. _Learn_ the headings, then all the details and diagrams. Then _cover the page_ and see what you can _scribble down_. Then try again and again until you can remember the whole lot. It's all just _easy marks to be won... or lost_.

Reflection

The Ripple Tank is Really Good for Displaying Waves

Learn all these diagrams showing _reflection of waves_. They could ask you to complete _any one of them_ in the Exam. It can be quite a bit _trickier_ than you think unless you've _practised_ them real well _beforehand_.

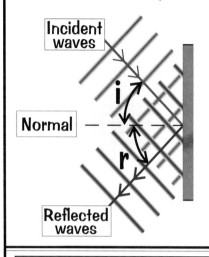

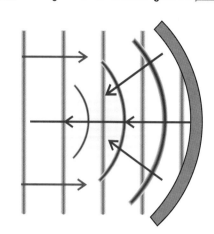

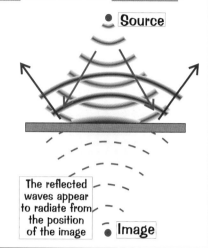

The reflected waves appear to radiate from the position of the image ● Image

Reflection of Light

Reflection of light is what allows us to _SEE_ objects.
When light reflects from an _even_ surface (_smooth and shiny_ like a _mirror_) then it's all reflected at the _same angle_ and you get a _clear reflection_.
Sound also reflects off _hard surfaces_ in the form of _echoes_.
Reflection of light and of sound gives evidence that light and sound travel as waves.
And don't forget, _THE LAW OF REFLECTION_ applies to _every reflected ray_:

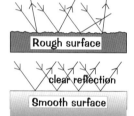

Angle of **_INCIDENCE_** = Angle of **_REFLECTION_**

Reflection In a Plane Mirror — How to Locate The Image

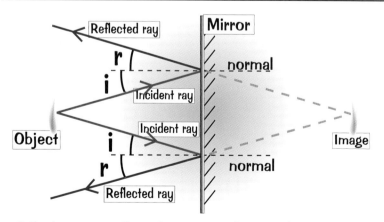

You need to be able to _reproduce_ this entire diagram of _how an image is formed_ in a _PLANE MIRROR_.
Learn these _two_ important points:

1) The _image_ is the _SAME SIZE_ as the _object_.
2) It is _AS FAR BEHIND_ the mirror as the object is _in front_.

1) To draw _any reflected ray_, just make sure the _angle of reflection_, r, equals the _angle of incidence_, i.
2) Note that these two angles are _ALWAYS_ defined between the ray itself and the dotted _NORMAL_.
3) _Don't ever_ label them as the angle between the ray and the _surface_. Definitely uncool.

Learn reflection thoroughly — try to look at it from all sides...

First make sure you can draw all those diagrams from memory. Then make sure you've learnt the rest well enough to answer typical meany Exam questions like these: _"Explain why you can see a piece of paper"_ _"Why is the image in a plane mirror virtual?"_

Refraction

1) _Refraction_ is when waves change _direction_ as they enter a _different medium_.
2) This is caused _entirely_ by the _change in speed_ of the waves.
3) It also causes the _wavelength_ to change, but remember that the _frequency_ does _not_ change.

1) Refraction _is Shown by Waves in a Ripple Tank Slowing Down_

1) The waves travel _slower_ in _shallower water_, causing _refraction_ as shown.
2) There's a change in _direction_, and a change in _wavelength_ but _NO change_ in _frequency_.

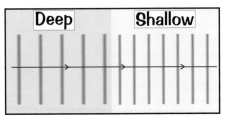 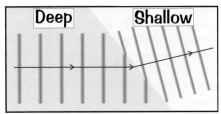

2) Refraction of Light — _The Good Old Glass Block Demo_

You can't fail to remember the old _"ray of light through a rectangular glass block"_ trick. Make sure you can draw this diagram _from memory_, with every detail _perfect_.

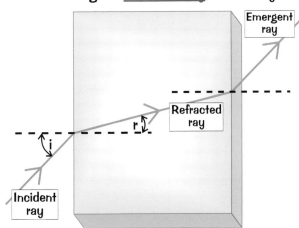

1) _Take careful note_ of the positions of the _normals_ and the _exact positions_ of the angles of _incidence_ and _refraction_ (and note it's the angle of _refraction_ — not _reflection_).
2) Most important of all remember _which way_ the ray _bends_.
3) The ray bends _towards_ the normal as it enters the _denser medium_, and _away_ from the normal as it _emerges_ into the _less dense_ medium.
4) Try to _visualise_ the shape of the _wiggle_ in the diagram — that can be easier than remembering the rule in words.

3) Refraction _Is always Caused By the Waves Changing Speed_

1) When waves _slow down_ they bend _towards_ the normal.
2) When _light_ enters _glass_ it _slows down_ to about _2/3_ of its normal speed (in air) i.e. it slows down to about _2 × 10⁸ m/s_ rather than _3 × 10⁸ m/s_.
3) When waves hit the boundary _along a normal_, i.e. at _exactly 90°_, then there will be _no change_ in direction. That's pretty important to remember, because they often _sneak_ it into a question somewhere. There'll still be a change in _speed_ and _wavelength_, though.
4) _Some_ light is also _reflected_ when light hits a _different medium_ such as glass.

4) Sound also Refracts but it's Hard to Spot

Sound will also refract (change direction) as it enters _different media_. However, since sound is always _spreading out so much_, the change in direction is _hard to spot_ under normal circumstances. But just remember, _sound does refract_, OK? The fact that sound and light are both refracted gives _further evidence_ that they travel as _waves_.

Revise Refraction — _but don't let it slow you down..._

The first thing you've gotta do is make sure you can spot the difference between the words _refraction_ and _reflection_. After that you need to _learn all this stuff about refraction_ — so you know exactly what it is. Make sure you know all those _diagrams_ inside out. _Cover and scribble_.

Refraction: Two Special Cases

Dispersion Produces Rainbows

1) _Different colours_ of light are _refracted_ by _different amounts_.
2) This is because they travel at _slightly different speeds_ in any given _medium_.
3) A _prism_ can be used to make the different colours of white light emerge at _different angles_.
4) This produces a _spectrum_ showing all the colours of the _rainbow_. This effect is called _DISPERSION_.

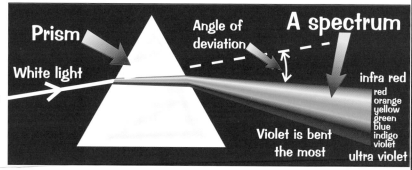

5) You need to know that _red light_ is refracted the _least_ — and _violet_ is refracted the _most_.
6) Also know the _order_ of colours in between: Red Orange Green Blue Indigo Violet
   which is remembered by: Richard Of ork ave Battle In Vain
   They may well test whether you can put them correctly into the diagram.
7) Also learn where _infrared_ and _ultraviolet_ light would appear if you could detect them.

Total Internal Reflection and The Critical Angle

1) This _only_ happens when _light_ is _coming out_ of something _dense_ like _glass_ or _water_ or _perspex_.
2) If the _angle_ is _shallow enough_ the ray _won't come out at all_, but it _reflects_ back into the glass (or whatever).   This is called _total internal reflection_ because _ALL_ of the light _reflects back in_.
3) You definitely need to learn this set of _THREE DIAGRAMS_ which show the three conditions:

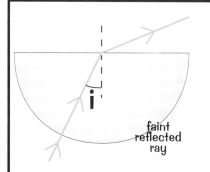

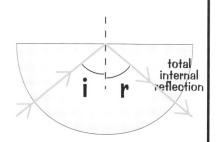

Angle of Incidence LESS than the Critical Angle.
Most of the light _passes through_ into the air but a _little_ bit of it is _internally reflected_.

Angle of Incidence EQUAL TO the Critical Angle.
The emerging ray comes out _along the surface_. There's quite a bit of _internal reflection_.

Angle of Incidence GREATER than the Critical Angle.
No light comes out.
It's _all_ internally reflected, i.e. _total internal reflection_.

1) The _Critical Angle_ for _glass_ is about 42°. This is _very handy_ because it means _45° angles_ can be used to get _total internal reflection_ as in the _prisms_ in the _binoculars_ and _periscope_ shown on the next page.
2) In _DIAMOND_ the _Critical Angle_ is much _lower_, about 24°. This is the reason why diamonds _sparkle_ so much, because there are lots of _internal reflections_.

Revision — sure it's Critical, but it's not a prism sentence...

First and foremost make sure you can _scribble all the diagrams_ down with all the details. Then _scribble a mini-essay_ for each topic, jotting down everything you can remember. Then check back and see what you _missed_. Then _learn the stuff you forgot_ and _try again_. Ahh... such fun.

Total Internal Reflection

Binoculars

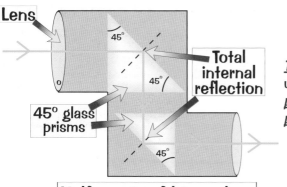

Lens

45°

45°

Total internal reflection

45° glass prisms

45°

Half a pair of binoculars

Periscope

Total internal reflection

Total Internal Reflection is used in *binoculars* and *periscopes*. Both use *45° prisms*.

Binoculars and *periscope* use prisms because they give slightly *better reflection* than a *mirror* would and they're also *easier* to hold accurately *in place*. Learn the exact *positioning* of the prisms. They could ask you to *complete* a diagram of a binocular or periscope and unless you've *practised* beforehand you'll find it *pretty tricky* to draw the prisms in *properly*.

Optical Fibres — Communications and Endoscopes

1) *Optical fibres* can carry *information* over *long distances* by repeated *total internal reflections*.
2) Optical communications have several *advantages* over *electrical signals* in wires:
   a) the signal doesn't need *boosting* as often.
   b) a cable of the *same diameter* can carry a lot *more information*.
   c) the signals cannot be *tapped into*, or suffer *interference* from electrical sources.
3) Normally no light whatever would be lost at each reflection. However some light *is lost* due to *imperfections* in the surface, so it still needs *boosting* every *few km*.

The fibre must be *narrow enough* to keep the angles *above* the critical angle, as shown, so the fibre mustn't be bent *too sharply* anywhere.

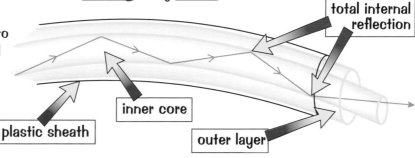

total internal reflection

plastic sheath

inner core

outer layer

Endoscopes are Used to Look Inside People

This is a *narrow bunch* of *optical fibres* with a *lens system* at each end. Another bunch of optical fibres carries light down *inside* to see with.
The image is displayed as a *full colour moving image* on a TV screen. Real impressive stuff. This means they can do operations *without* cutting big holes in people. This was never possible before optical fibres.

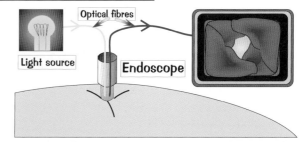

Optical fibres

Light source

Endoscope

Total Internal Reflection — sounds like a Government Inquiry...

Three sections to learn here, with diagrams for each. They always have *at least one* of these applications of total internal reflection in the Exam. *Learn them all*. None of this is difficult — but just make sure you've got all those little picky details firmly fastened inside your head.

The EM Spectrum

There are Seven Basic Types of Electromagnetic Wave

We split Electromagnetic waves (EM waves) into _seven_ basic types as shown below.
These EM waves form a _continuous spectrum_ so the different regions do actually _merge_ into each other.

RADIO WAVES	MICRO WAVES	INFRA RED	VISIBLE LIGHT	ULTRA VIOLET	X-RAYS	GAMMA RAYS
$1m$-$10^4 m$	$10^{-2} m$ (3cm)	$10^{-5} m$ (0.01mm)	$10^{-7} m$	$10^{-8} m$	$10^{-10} m$	$10^{-12} m$

Our _eyes_ can only detect a _very narrow range_ of EM waves which are the ones we call (visible) _light_.
All EM waves travel at _exactly_ the same _speed_ as light in a _vacuum_, and _pretty much_ the same speed
as light in _other media_ like glass or water — though this is always _slower_ than their speed in vacuum.

As the Wavelength Changes, So Do The Properties

1) As the _wavelength_ of EM radiation changes, its _interaction_ with matter changes. In particular the way
   any EM wave is _absorbed_, _reflected_ or _transmitted_ by any given substance depends _entirely_ on its
   wavelength — that's the whole point of these three pages of course!
2) When _any_ EM radiation is _absorbed_ it can cause _two effects_:
       a) _Heating_   b) Creation of a _tiny alternating current_ with the _same_ frequency as the radiation.
3) You need to know all the details that follow about all the different part of the EM spectrum:

Radio Waves are Used Mainly For Communications

1) _Radio Waves_ are used mainly for _communication_.
2) Both _TV and FM Radio_ use _short wavelength_ radio waves of about
   1m wavelength.
3) To receive these wavelengths you need to be more or less in _direct
   sight_ of the transmitter, because they will _not_ bend (diffract) over
   hills or travel very far _through_ buildings.
4) The _longer wavelengths_ can travel further because they are
   reflected from an _electrically charged layer_ in the Earth's upper atmosphere (the ionosphere).
   This means they can be sent further around the Earth.

Microwaves Are Used For Cooking and Satellite Signals

1) _Microwaves_ have _two_ main uses:
   cooking food and _satellite_ transmissions.
2) Satellite transmissions use a frequency of microwaves
   which _passes easily_ through the _Earth's atmosphere_,
   including _clouds_, which seems pretty sensible.

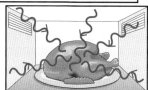

3) The frequency used for _cooking_, on the other hand is one which is readily _absorbed_ by _water
   molecules_. The microwaves pass easily _into the food_ and are then _absorbed_ by the _water molecules_
   and turn into heat _inside_ the food.
4) Microwaves can therefore be _dangerous_ because they can be absorbed by _living tissue_ and the heat
   will _damage or kill_ the cells causing a sort of _"cold burn"_.

The spectrum — isn't that something kinda rude in Biology...

There are lots of details on this page that you definitely need to know. The top diagram is an
absolute must — they usually give it you with one or two missing labels to be filled in. _Learn_
the four sections on this page then _scribble_ a _mini-essay_ for each one to see what you know.

The EM Spectrum

Visible light *is Used To See With and In Optical Fibres*

Visible Light is pretty useful. It's used in *Optical Fibre Digital Communications* and endoscopes which are the best ones for your answer *in the Exam* (see P.81).

Infrared Radiation — *Toasters and Remote Controls*

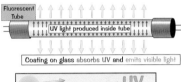

1) *Infrared* (or IR) is otherwise known as *heat radiation*. This is given out by all *hot objects* and you *feel it* on your *skin* as *radiant heat*. Infrared is readily *absorbed* by *all* materials and *causes heating*.

2) *Radiant heaters* (i.e. those that *glow red*) use infrared radiation, including *toasters* and *grills*.

3) *Over-exposure* to infrared causes *damage* to cells. This is what causes *sunburn*.

4) Infrared is also used for all the *remote controls* of *TV's and videos*.

Ultraviolet Light *Causes Skin Cancer*

1) This is what causes *skin cancer* if you spend *too much time* in the *sun*.

2) It also causes your skin to *tan*. *Sunbeds* give out UV rays but *less harmful ones* than the Sun does.

3) *Darker skin* protects against UV rays by *preventing* them from reaching more vulnerable *skin tissues* deeper down.

4) There are special *coatings* which *absorb* UV light and then *give out visible light* instead. These are used to coat the inside of *fluorescent tubes* and lamps.

5) Ultra violet is also useful for hidden *security marks* which are written in special ink that can only be seen with an ultraviolet light.

X-Rays *Are Used in Hospitals, but are Pretty Dangerous*

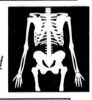

1) These are used in *hospitals* to take *X-ray photographs* of people to see whether they have any *broken bones*.

2) X-rays pass easily through *flesh* but not through *denser material* such as *bones* or *metal*.

3) X-rays can cause *cancer*, so *radiographers*, who take X-ray pictures *all day long* wear *lead aprons* and stand behind a *lead screen* to keep their *exposure* to X-rays to a *minimum*.

Gamma Rays *Cause Cancer but Are Used to Treat it Too*

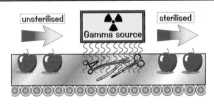

1) Gamma Rays are used to kill *harmful bacteria* in food to keep it *fresher for longer*.

2) They are also used to *sterilise medical instruments*, again by *killing the bacteria*.

3) They can also be used in the *treatment of cancer* because they *kill cancer cells*.

4) Gamma rays tend to *pass through* soft tissue but *some* are *absorbed* by the cells.

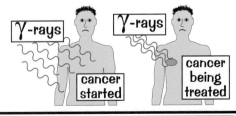

5) In *high doses*, Gamma rays (along with X-rays and UV rays) can *kill normal cells*.

6) In *lower doses* all these three types of EM Waves can cause normal cells to become *cancerous*.

Radiographers are like Teachers — *they can see right through you...*

Here are the other five parts of the EM spectrum for you to learn. Ace, isn't it. At least there's some groovy diagrams to help relieve the tedium. On this page there are five sections.

Do a *mini-essay* for each section, then *check*, *re-learn*, *re-scribble*, *re-check*, etc. etc.

Sound Waves

1) Sound travels as a wave:

Sound can be _reflected_ off walls (echoes), it can be _refracted_ as it passes into different media and it can _diffract_ around doors. These are all standard properties of waves so we deduce that _sound travels as a wave_. This "sound" reasoning can also be applied to deduce the wave nature of light.

2) Sound Waves Travel at Various Speeds in Different Media

1) _Sound Waves_ are caused by _vibrating_ objects.
2) Sound waves are _longitudinal_ waves, which travel at _fixed speeds_ in particular _media_, as shown in the table.
3) As you can see, the _denser_ the medium, the _faster_ sound travels through it, generally speaking anyway.
4) Sound generally travels _faster in solids_ than in liquids, and faster in liquids than in gases.

Substance	Density	Speed of Sound
Iron	7.9 g/cm³	5000 m/s
Rubber	0.9 g/cm³	1600 m/s
Water	1.0 g/cm³	1400 m/s
Cork	0.3 g/cm³	500 m/s
Air	0.001 g/cm³	330 m/s

3) Sound Doesn't Travel Through Vacuum

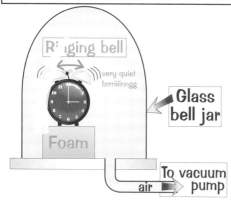

Ringing bell

very quiet brrriiiinngg

Glass bell jar

Foam

To vacuum pump

air

1) Sound waves can be _reflected_, _refracted_ and _diffracted_.
2) But one thing they _can't do_ is travel through a _vacuum_.
3) This is nicely demonstrated by the jolly old _bell jar experiment_.
4) As the air is _sucked out_ by the _vacuum pump_, the sound gets _quieter and quieter_.
5) The bell has to be _mounted_ on something like _foam_ to stop the sound from it travelling through the solid surface and making the bench vibrate, because you'd hear that instead.

4) Echoes and Reverberation are due to REFLECTED Sound

1) Sound will only be _reflected_ from _hard flat surfaces_. Things like _carpets_ and _curtains_ act as _absorbing surfaces_ which will _absorb_ sounds rather than reflect them.
2) This is very noticeable in the _reverberation_ in an _empty room_. A big empty room sounds _completely different_ once you've put carpet and curtains in, and a bit of furniture, because these things absorb the sound quickly and stop it _echoing_ (reverberating) around the room.

5) Amplitude is a Measure of the Energy Carried by Any Wave

1) The greater the _AMPLITUDE_, the _more ENERGY_ the wave carries.
2) In _SOUND_ this means it'll be _LOUDER_.
3) _Bigger amplitude_ means a _louder sound_.
4) With _LIGHT_, a bigger amplitude means it'll be _BRIGHTER_.

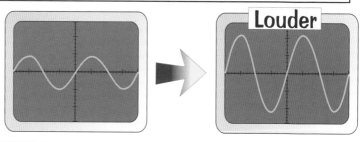

Louder

If sound travelled through vacuum — sunny days would be deafening...

Once again the page is broken up into five sections with important numbered points for each. All those numbered points are important. They're all mentioned specifically in the syllabuses so you should expect them to test exactly this stuff in the Exams. _Learn and enjoy._

Frequency and Ultrasound

The Frequency of a Sound Wave Determines its Pitch

1) *High frequency sound waves* sound *HIGH PITCHED* like a *squeaking mouse*.
2) *Low frequency* sound waves sound *LOW PITCHED* like a *mooing cow*.
3) *Frequency* is the number of complete *vibrations* each second. It's measured in *Hertz*, *Hz*.
4) Other common units are *kHz* (1000 Hz) and *MHz* (1,000,000 Hz).
5) *High frequency* (or high pitch) also means *shorter wavelength*.
6) The range of frequencies heard by humans is from 20Hz to 20kHz.
7) These *CRO screens* are *very important* so make sure you know all about them:

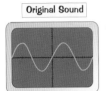
Original Sound

The CRO screens tell us about the *pitch* and *loudness* of the sound:

Higher pitched

1) The *closer* the peaks are together, the *higher* pitched the sound (and the *higher* the frequency).

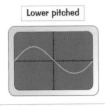
Lower pitched

Higher pitched and louder

2) When the peaks are *further apart* then the sound is at a *lower pitch* (a lower frequency).

3) The CRO screen will show *large peaks* for a *loud noise* (sound waves with a *big amplitude*).

Ultrasound is Sound with a Higher Frequency than We Can Hear

Electrical devices can be made which produce *electrical oscillations* of *any frequency*. These can easily be converted into *mechanical vibrations* to produce *sound* waves *beyond the range* of *human hearing* (i.e. frequencies above 20kHz). This is called *ULTRASOUND* and it has loads of uses:

1) Industrial Cleaning of Delicate mechanisms

1) *ULTRASOUND CAN BE USED TO CLEAN CASTINGS* without them having to be *dismantled*.
2) The alternatives would either *damage* the equipment or else it would need to be *dismantled* first.
3) The *same technique* is also be used by dentists to remove *layers of tartar* from teeth.

2) Industrial Quality Control

In industrial quality control Ultrasound can be used to *detect* faulty goods. Any *flaws or cracks* in the metal castings can be detected with the aid of the ultrasound.

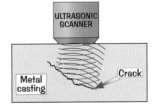

3) For Pre-Natal Scanning of a Foetus

This follows the *same principle* as the industrial quality control. The Ultrasound waves are used as a *safe alternative* to X-rays in order to discover if the foetus is healthy or not. The results are *processed* by *computer* to produce a *video image* of the foetus.

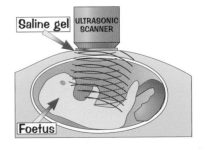

Types of Radiation

Don't get _mixed up_ between _nuclear_ radiation which is _dangerous_ — and _electromagnetic_ radiation which _generally isn't_. Gamma radiation is included in both, of course. A substance which gives out radiation all the time is called _radioactive_.

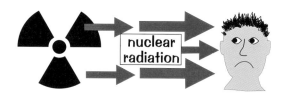 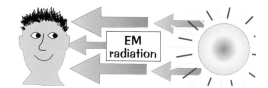

Nuclear Radiation: Alpha, Beta and Gamma (α, β and γ)

You need to remember _three things_ about _each type of radiation_:
1) What they actually _are_.
2) How well they _penetrate_ materials.
3) How strongly they _ionise_ that material. (i.e. bash into atoms and _knock electrons off_)
   There's a pattern: The _further_ the radiation can _penetrate_ before hitting an atom and getting stopped, the _less damage_ it will do along the way and so the _less ionising_ it is.

Alpha Particles are Helium Nuclei

1) They are relatively _big_ and _heavy_ and _slow moving_.
2) They therefore _don't_ penetrate into materials but are _stopped quickly_.
3) Because of their size they are _strongly_ ionising, which just means they _bash into_ a lot of atoms and _knock electrons off_ them before they slow down, which creates lots of ions — hence the term "_ionising_".

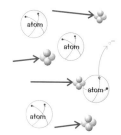

Beta Particles are Electrons

1) These are _in between_ alpha and gamma in terms of their _properties_.
2) They move _quite_ fast and they are _quite_ small (they're electrons).
3) They _penetrate moderately_ before colliding and are _moderately ionising_ too.
4) For every _β–particle_ emitted, a _neutron_ turns to a _proton_ in the nucleus.

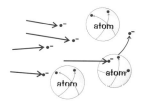

Gamma Rays are Very Short Wavelength EM Waves

1) They are the _opposite_ of alpha particles in a way.
2) They _penetrate a long way_ into materials without being stopped.
3) This means they are _weakly_ ionising because they tend to _pass through_ rather than colliding with atoms. Eventually they _hit something_ and do _damage_.

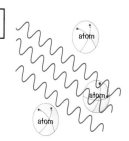

Learn the three types of radiation — it's easy as abc...

Alpha, beta and gamma. You do realise those are just the first three letters of the Greek alphabet don't you: α, β, γ — just like a, b, c. They might sound like complex names to you but they were just easy labels at the time. Anyway, _learn all the facts_ about them — and _scribble_.

Background Radiation

Remember What Blocks the Three Types of Radiation...

As radiation *passes through* materials some of the radiation is *absorbed*. The greater the *thickness* of material the *more absorption*.

They really like this for Exam questions, so make sure *you know* what it takes to *block* each of the *three*:

ALPHA particles are blocked by *paper*.
BETA particles are blocked by thin *aluminium*.
GAMMA rays are blocked by *thick lead*.

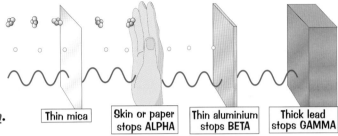

Thin mica | Skin or paper stops ALPHA | Thin aluminium stops BETA | Thick lead stops GAMMA

Of course anything *equivalent* will also block them, e.g. *skin* will stop *alpha*, but *not* the others; a thin sheet of *any metal* will stop *beta*; and *very thick concrete* will stop *gamma* just like lead does.

Background Radiation Comes From Many Sources

Natural background radiation comes from:

1) Radioactivity of naturally occurring *unstable isotopes* which are *all around us* — in the *air*, in *food*, in *building materials* and in the *rocks* under our feet.

2) Radiation from *space*, which is known as *cosmic rays*. These come mostly from the *Sun*.

3) Radiation due to *human activity*. i.e. *fallout* from *nuclear explosions* or *dumped nuclear waste*. But this represents a *tiny* proportion of the total background radiation.

The **RELATIVE PROPORTIONS** of *background radiation*:

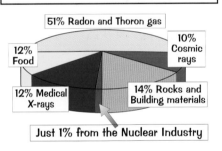

51% Radon and Thoron gas
10% Cosmic rays
12% Food
14% Rocks and Building materials
12% Medical X-rays
Just 1% from the Nuclear Industry

The Level of Background Radiation Changes, Depending on Where You Are

1) At *high altitudes* (e.g. in *jet planes*) it *increases* because of more exposure to *cosmic rays*.

2) *Underground in mines*, etc. it increases because of the *rocks* all around. Rocks like *granite* have a high background count rate.

3) Certain *underground rocks* can cause higher levels at the *surface*, especially if they release *radioactive radon gas*, which tends to get trapped *inside people's houses*. This varies widely across the UK depending on the *rock type*, as shown:

Millom

Coloured bits indicate more radiation from rocks

Background Radiation — it's no good burying your head in the sand...

Yip, it's funny old stuff is radiation, that's for sure. It is quite mysterious, I guess, but just like anything else, the *more you learn about it*, the *less* of a mystery it becomes. This page is positively bristling with simple straightforward facts about radiation. Three tiny little *mini-essays* practised two or three times and all this knowledge will be yours — forever. Enjoy. ☺

Radiation Uses & Hazards

Thickness Control in Industry and Manufacturing

This is a classic application and is _pretty popular in Exams_. It's really very simple.

1) You have a _radioactive source_ and you direct it _through_ the stuff being made, usually a continuous sheet of _paper_ or _cardboard_ or _metal_ etc.

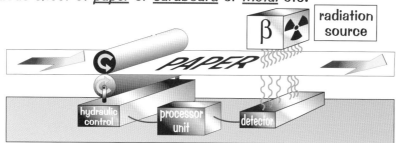

2) The _detector_ is on the _other side_ and is connected to a _control unit_.

3) When the amount of radiation detected _goes down_, it means the stuff is coming out _too thick_ and so the control unit _pinches the rollers up_ a bit to make it _thinner_ again.

4) If the reading _goes up_, it means it's _too thin_, so the control unit _opens the rollers out_ a bit.

Radioactive Dating of Rocks and Archaeological Specimens

1) The discovery of radioactivity and the idea of _half-life_ gave scientists their _first opportunity_ to _accurately_ work out the _age_ of _rocks_ and _fossils_ and archaeological specimens.

2) By measuring the _amount_ of a _radioactive isotope_ left in a sample, and knowing its _half-life_, you can work out _how long_ the thing has been around.

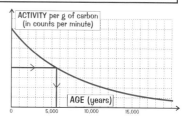

Radiation Harms Living Cells

1) _Alpha_, _beta_ and _gamma_ radiation will cheerfully enter living cells and _collide_ with molecules.

2) These collisions cause _ionisation_, which _damages_ or _destroys_ the molecules.

3) _Lower_ doses tend to cause _minor_ damage without _killing_ the cell.

4) This can give rise to _mutant_ cells which divide _uncontrollably_. This is _cancer_.

5) _Higher_ doses tend to _kill cells_ completely, which causes _radiation sickness_ if a lot of your body cells _all get blatted at once_.

6) The _extent_ of the harmful effects depends on _two things_:
   a) How much _exposure_ you have to the radiation.
   b) The _energy_ and _penetration_ of the radiation emitted, since some types are _more hazardous_ than others, of course.

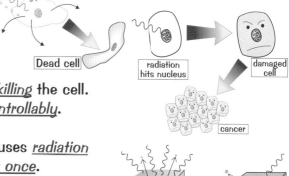

Radiotherapy — the Treatment of Cancer Using γ-Rays

Since high doses of gamma rays will _kill all living cells_ they can be used to _treat cancers_. The gamma rays have to be directed _carefully_ and at just the right _dosage_ so as to kill the _cancer cells_ without damaging too many _normal cells_.

Radiation Sickness — well yes, it does all get a bit tedious...

Quite a few picky details here. It's easy to kid yourself that you don't really need to know all this stuff. Well take it from me, you _do_ need to know it all and there's only one surefire way to find out whether you do or not. Four _mini-essays_ please, with all the picky details in. Enjoy.

Atomic Structure

See the Chemistry Book for a few more details on this.

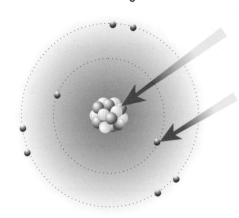

The _NUCLEUS_ contains _protons_ and _neutrons_.
Most of the _MASS_ of the atom is contained in the _nucleus_, but it takes up virtually _no space_ — it's _tiny_.

The _ELECTRONS_ fly around the _outside_.
They're _negatively charged_ and really really _small_.
They occupy _a lot of space_ and this gives the atom its _overall size_, even though it's mostly _empty space_.
The number of electrons is _equal to_ the number of protons.
This means that the whole atom has _no overall charge_.

Make sure you _learn this table_:

PARTICLE	MASS	CHARGE
Proton	1	+1
Neutron	1	0
Electron	$\frac{1}{2000}$	-1

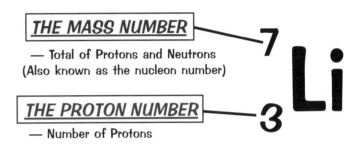

THE MASS NUMBER
— Total of Protons and Neutrons
(Also known as the nucleon number)

THE PROTON NUMBER
— Number of Protons

$^{7}_{3}\text{Li}$

Isotopes are Different Forms of The Same Element

1) All atoms of a _particular element_ have the _same number_ of protons.
2) _Isotopes_ are atoms with the _SAME_ number of protons but a _DIFFERENT_ number of neutrons.
3) Hence they have the _same proton number_, but _different mass number_.
4) _Carbon-12 and Carbon-14_ are good examples:
5) _Most elements_ have different isotopes but there's usually only one or two _stable_ ones.
6) Radioisotopes are _radioactive isotopes_, which means they _decay_ into other _elements_ and give out _radiation_.
This is where all _radioactivity_ comes from —
unstable radioactive isotopes undergoing nuclear _decay_ and spitting out _high energy_ particles.

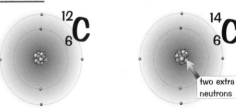

$^{12}_{6}\text{C}$ $^{14}_{6}\text{C}$

two extra neutrons

Rutherford's Scattering and The Demise of the Plum Pudding

1) In 1804 _John Dalton_ said matter was made up of tiny _solid spheres_ which he called _atoms_.
2) Later they discovered _electrons_ could be _removed_ from atoms. They then saw atoms as _spheres_ of _positive charge_ with tiny negative electrons _stuck in them_ like plums in a _plum pudding_.
3) Then _Ernest Rutherford_ and his merry men tried firing _alpha particles_ at a _thin gold foil_. Most of them just went _straight through_, but the odd one came straight _back at them_, which was frankly a bit of a _shocker_ for Ernie and his pals.
Being pretty clued up guys though they realised this meant that _most_ of the mass of the atom was concentrated _at the centre_ in a _tiny nucleus_, with a _positive charge_.
This means that most of an atom is just made up of _empty space_, which is also _a bit of a shocker_ when you think about it.

Gold Foil

Alpha source

Detector

Plum Pudding Theory — by 1911 they'd had their fill of it...

Yeah, that's right — atoms are mostly empty space. When you think about it, those electrons are amazing little jokers really. They have almost no mass, no size, and a tiny little −ve charge. In the end it's only their frantic whizzing about that makes atoms what they are. It's outrageous.

Revision Summary for Module Twelve

One thing's for sure — there are loads of fairly easy facts to learn about waves and radiation. Of course there are still some bits which need thinking about, but most of it is fairly easy stuff which just needs learning. Don't forget, this book contains all the important information which they've specifically mentioned in the syllabus, and this is precisely the stuff they're going to test you on in the Exams. You must practise these questions over and over again until they're easy.

1) Sketch a wave and mark on it the amplitude and wavelength.
2) Define frequency, amplitude and wavelength for a wave.
3) Give three examples of waves carrying energy.
4) Sketch the patterns when plane ripples reflect at a) a plane surface, b) a curved surface.
5) What is the law of reflection? Are sound and light reflected?
6) Draw a neat ray diagram to show how to locate the position of the image in a plane mirror.
7) What is refraction? What causes it? How does it affect wavelength and frequency?
8) Sketch a ray of light going through a rectangular glass block, showing the angles i and r.
9) How fast does light go in glass? Which way does it bend as it enters glass? What if i=90°?
10) What is dispersion? Sketch the diagram which illustrates it with all the labels.
11) Sketch the three diagrams to illustrate Total Internal Reflection and the Critical Angle.
12) Sketch two applications of total internal reflection which use 45° prisms, and explain them.
13) Give details of the two main uses of optical fibres. How do optical fibres work?
14) What aspect of EM waves determines their differing properties?
15) Sketch the EM spectrum with all its details. What happens when EM waves are absorbed?
16) Give full details of the uses of radio waves.
17) Give full details of the two main uses of microwaves, and the three main uses of infrared.
18) Give a sensible example of the use of visible light. What is its main use?
19) Detail three uses of UV light, two uses of X-rays and three uses of gamma rays.
20) What harm will UV, X-rays and gamma rays do in __high__ doses? What about in __low__ doses?
21) What's an echo? What is reverberation? What affects reverberation in a room?
22) What's the connection between amplitude and the energy carried by a wave?
23) What effect does greater amplitude have on a) sound waves   b) light waves?
24) What's the relationship between frequency and pitch for a sound wave?
25) Sketch CRO screens showing higher and lower pitch and quiet and loud sounds.
26) What is ultrasound? Give details of two applications of ultrasound.
27) Describe in detail the nature and properties of the three types of radiation: α, β, and γ.
28) How do the three types compare in penetrating power and ionising power?
29) List several things which will block each of the three types.
30) Sketch a fairly accurate pie chart to show the six main sources of background radiation.
31) List three places where the level of background radiation is increased and explain why.
32) Sketch an atom. Give three details about the nucleus and the electrons.
33) Draw up a wee table detailing the mass and charge of the three basic subatomic particles.
34) Explain what the mass number and proton number of an atom represent.
35) Write down the number of electrons, protons and neutrons there are in an atom of $^{226}_{88}Ra$,
   and say what its overall charge would be.
36) Explain what isotopes are. Give an example. Are most isotopes stable or unstable?
37) What was the Plum Pudding Model? Who put paid to that crazy old idea?
38) Describe Rutherford's Scattering Experiment with a diagram and say what happened?
39) What was the inevitable conclusion to be drawn from this experiment?

Answers

P.35 1) Cu = 64, K = 39, Kr = 84, Fe = 56, Cl = 35.5   2) NaOH = 40, Fe_2O_3 = 160, C_6H_{12} = 86, $Mg(NO_3)_2$ = 148   __P.36 Revn Sumy__   27a) 40 b) 108 c) 44 d) 84 e) 106
f) 81 g) 56 h) 17 i) 58 j) 58.5 28a) 40.0% b)i) 12.0% ii) 27.3% iii) 75.0% c)i) 74.2% ii) 70.0% iii) 52.9%
__P.58__ 1) $Fe_2O_3(s) + 3H_2 (g) \rightarrow 2Fe (s) + 3H_2O (l)$ 2) $6HCl (aq) + 2Al (s) \rightarrow 2AlCl_3 (aq) + 3H_2 (g)$
__P.59 Revn Sumy__   43) a) $O_2 (g) + 2H_2 (g) \rightarrow 2H_2O (l)$ b) $2Li (s) + 2H_2O (l) \rightarrow 2LiOH (aq) + H_2 (g)$
__P.76 Revn Sumy__   2) 0.09m/s, 137m   __4)__ 35m/s² __20)__ 6420J

Index

A

absorbing 77, 81
acceleration 60-62, 64, 65, 66
ace 42, 47
acid 24, 34, 53
acid rain 9
activation energy 27
air 38, 43, 53
air resistance 65
airships 50
alcohol 31
alkali 34, 56
alkali metal oxides 53
alkali metals 51, 53
alkaline 52, 53
allele 14
alpha particles/emission 86, 88
alternating current. *See* AC
aluminium 43, 55
aluminium chloride 55
amber 19
ammonia 33, 34, 39
ammonium nitrate fertiliser 34
amplitude 77, 84
angles of incidence/reflection and refraction 78, 79
animal characteristics 13
anions 45
anti diuretic hormone. *See* ADH
aphids 4
aquaplaning 67
aqueous 58
arctic circle 72
arctic creatures 2
areas of pistons 71
argon 42, 43, 50
artificial selection 16
atmosphere 7
atom 41, 42, 43, 45
atomic mass 46
atomic number 35, 41, 47
atomic structure 89
atoms 35, 40, 45, 59
attraction 44, 75

B

background radiation 20, 87
bacteria 7, 15, 30, 31, 34
balanced forces 62
beer and wine 31
bell jar experiment 84
beta particles/emission 86, 88
big problems 8
big rotating ball 72
big scary names 35
binoculars 81
biomass pyramids 6
birth rate 8
bleach 29, 56
body temperature 2
bogs 18
boiling 38, 44
bomb 24
bouncing 37
brakes 66, 67
braking distance 67
bread-making 31
break 27
breaking bonds 38
breeding 16
brewing 31
bright specks 39

brine 56
broken bones 83
bromine 39, 52, 54, 55, 57
Brownian motion 39
bumping 39
burn 53
burning 32

C

caesium 51
calcium 44
calcium chloride 45
camouflage 3
cancer 20, 83, 88
car brakes 71
carbon 35
carbon dioxide 7, 9, 29, 31, 43
carbon tetrachloride 54
carbon-12 41
carbon-14 41
carcinogens 20
carnivore 4
cars 9
cat 11
catalyst 24, 27, 28, 30, 33, 49
catalytic converters 9
caterpillars 4
cations 45
cell nucleus 13, 14
changes of state 38
characteristics 16, 20
charged particles 44
checkerboard 21
chemical behaviour 41
chemical bonds 44
chemical equations 58
chemicals 20
chlorine 29, 44, 45, 52, 54, 55, 56
chromium 49
chromosomes 13, 14, 21
circular barrier/ripples 78
clones 15
clouds of dust 75
cobalt 49
cobalt chloride paper 29
cold! 50
collide 37
collision theory 26
colours 80
comets 74
common sense 3
communications 74, 81, 82
competition 1
compost heaps 7
compound 35, 43
compressed 37
concentration 24, 26
condenser 33
conduct electricity 44
constellations 74
consumer 4
contraception 8
cooking food 82
cooling graphs 38
Copernicus 74
copper 43, 49
copper sulphate 29
copper(II) sulphate 32
corrosive 29
cosmic rays 87
covalent 54

covalent Bonds 45
critical angle 80, 81
CRO displays 85
crude oil 33
crystals 44, 53
cuboid 44
cyanide 29
cycle 22

D

daffodils 15
Dalton, John 89
damaging surfaces 70
dandelions 6
dangerous 82, 83
dating of rocks 88
days and seasons 72
dead plants or animals 17
death rate 8
decay microbes 19
deceleration 61, 67
decomposition 4, 7
dense 80
denser 79, 83, 84
density 37, 49, 50, 51, 70
depth, pressure 70
desert creatures 2
diffraction 82
diffuse 39
diffusion experiments 39
dinosaurs 16
disease 1
disease-resistance 16
dispersion 80
dissolve 39, 44, 52
distance-time graphs 61
Dmitri 46
DNA 13, 14
dominant 13, 20
dosage of radiation 83
double helix 13
drag 65, 66
drawing pins 70
drivelly facts 10
dust 75

E

Earth 73
Earth's atmosphere 82
echoes 77, 84
ecosystem 9
effects of environment 12
egg cells 13, 22
elastic limit 69
elastic potential energy 69
electrical discharge tubes 50
electrical oscillations 85
electrolysis 56
electromagnetic waves/ radiation/spectrum 73, 82, 86
electron 45, 51
electron arrangements 48
electron configurations 42
electron shell rules 42
electron shells 42, 47

electrons 40, 41, 42, 45, 46, 47, 89
elements 35, 41, 43, 45, 46, 48, 89
elliptical, orbits 73
EM spectrum 20
EM waves/radiation 73, 86
emissions 8
endoscopes 81
endothermic reaction 32
energy 77
energy levels 42
energy, of waves 84
environment 16
environmental damage 9
environmental variation 11
enzymes 30, 31
equations 58
eutrophication 34
evaporate 38, 39, 56
evolution 17
exhaust gases 9
exothermic 34
exothermic reaction 32
expand 37
explosion 24
exposure, radiation 83, 88
extension 69
extinction 17

F

female menstrual cycle 22
fermentation 31
fertilisation 21
fertilised egg 22
fertilisers 33
fizzing 52
flame 53
flammable 29
flat spots 38
fleas 6
fluorescent tubes 83
fluorine 52, 54, 56
foetus, ultrasound 85
follicle stimulating hormone. *See* FSH
food 30, 31, 68, 87
food chains 4
food energy 4
food webs 4
force, area, pressure 70
force diagrams 62, 65
force multipliers 71
force of attraction 37, 64, 74
forces 38
formula 35
formula triangle 60
fossil fuels 9
fossils 17, 18
fossils, dating of 88
foundations, pressure 70
foxes 3, 6
francium 51
free-fallers, terminal velocity 66
freezing 30, 38
frequency 77
frequency, of waves 79, 85
friction 65, 66, 68
frogs 5
fuels 32
full cycle 77
full outer shell 45
full shell 44, 47

fume cupboard 54
fun guy 7
fungi 7
funny old stuff 70

G

galaxies 75
gamete 13
gametes 21
gamma sources/emission 83, 86, 88
gas 37-39, 43, 50, 54
gas syringe 25
gene 11, 13, 14
gene types 21
genetic variation 11
genetics 13
giant ionic lattices 53
giant ionic structures 44, 53
girl or boy? 21
glaciers 19
glass block demo 79
glowing splint 29
grand canyon 19
gravity 64, 65, 74, 75
grazers 1
group 47, 50, 51, 54
group O 50
group Seven 44
group Six 44

H

Haber process 33, 56
halogens 54, 56
harmful/harmless 29, 83
hazards 67, 88
HCl 54, 56
hearing 85
heat radiation 83
heat/heat energy 38, 73, 75, 82
heating graph 38
helium 35, 50
helium nuclei 86
herbivore 4
herons 5
hideously easy 4, 6, 64
high doses 83, 88
holes in food webs 5
hoof 17
horse 17
how dopey you are 67
Hubble telescope 74
hump 2
Huntington's chorea 20
hydraulics, jacks, brakes 71
hydrogen 7, 29 33, 52, 56
hydrogen chloride 54
hydroxide 52, 53

I

ice skates, pressure 70
image, in plane mirror 78
incidence, angle of 78, 79
industrial reactions 28
inert gases 50
information 81
infra-red (or IR) 80, 83
instant regurgitation 76
iodine 52, 54, 55, 57
ionic 53, 54
ionic bonds 44, 45
ionic compounds 45, 51, 53

Index

ionisation 86, 88
ions 40, 44, 45
iron 28, 43, 49, 55
iron sulphide 43
iron(III) bromide 55
irritant 29
Isaac Newton 62
isotopes 41, 89

J

joules 68
Jupiter 73

K

kill cells, radiation 82, 88
kinetic energy 68
krypton 50

L

lab tests 29
lactic acid 31
lactose 31
large surface area 2
lasers 50
lattice 37, 44
law of reflection 78
laws of motion,three 62
light 78
light bulbs 50
limewater 29
lion 3
liquid 37, 39, 54, 58
lithium 51, 52
litmus paper 29, 56
load 69
longitudinal waves 84
loud noise, amplitude 84
lower doses 83, 88
lubricants 66
luteinising hormone.
        See LH

M

magnesium oxide 45, 58
male or female 21
manganese 49
margarine 56
Mars 73
mass 35, 40, 41,
        64, 68, 74
mass balance 25
mass number 35,41, 89
master piston, hydraulics 71
matter 37
maximum speed 66
media, for waves 79, 80,
        82, 84
medium 77
melting 38, 44
melting points 44
menstrual cycle 23
Mercury 73
metal halides 55
metals 45, 47, 49, 51, 55
methane 33
microscope 39, 40
Milky Way galaxy 75
minnows 5
missing links 17
mixture 39, 43
modern farming 8, 16
molecular compounds 54
molecules 37, 38, 39, 54

molten 44
monatomic 50
Moon 64
moons 74
mostly empty space 75, 89
mucus 20
multiple births 22
mutagens 20
mutant cells, cancer 88

N

natural gas 33
natural satellites 74
negatively charged 40
neon 50
Neptune 73
neutral atom 40
neutral salt 34, 52
neutralisation 32, 34
neutrons 40,41, 89
Newlands' Octaves 46
Newtons 64
nickel 49
nitrates 7, 34
nitric acid 28, 34
nitrogen 33, 42-43
nitrogen monoxide 34
nitrogen oxides 9
noble gases 50
non-metals 45, 54
normal, light rays 78, 79
northern hemisphere 72
nuclear decay 89
nuclear radiation 20, 86
nuclear waste 87
nucleus 14, 40, 41, 42
nucleus/nuclei 89
number pyramid 6

O

offspring 21
old rogue 46, 59
omnivore 4
opposite charges 44
optical fibres 81, 83
orbits 40, 64, 73, 74, 75
organic matter 7
outer shell 42, 45
outward characteristics 15
ovary 22
oxides, oxidising 29, 34, 53
oxygen 7,29, 43, 44

P

parachute 66
particles 40
Pascal, Pa 71
penetration, radiation 86
percentage mass 35
perch 5
periodic table 35, 44,
        46-47
periods 47
periscopes 81
perspex 80
petrification 18
petrol 29
pH indicator 52
photographic film 57
photosynthesis 7, 32
physical state 58
physical types 21
pike 5

pitch, sound waves 85
plane mirror 78
plane waves 78
planets 73, 74, 75
plants 7
platinum catalyst 28, 34
plum pudding 89
Pluto 73
poisonous 9, 54
polar bear 2
pollen grains 39
positive charge 40
potassium 44, 51, 52
potassium
        manganate(VII) 39
potato 15
power stations 9
pre-natal scanning 85
precipitate 25, 55
predator 1, 3
pressure 26, 33, 37, 70, 71
pressure in liquids 70, 71
prey 3
primary consumer 4
prisms 80, 81
producer 4
products 25
proportional 69
protein 30
proton number 41, 89
protons 40-41, 46, 89
pyramids 6

Q

quality control 85

R

rabbits 3, 4, 6
radiation 20
radiation hazards 88
radiation, heat 75, 82
radiation, nuclear 86
radiation sickness 88
radio waves 82
radioactivity, radio-isotopes,
        etc 89
radiographers, X-rays 83
radiotherapy 88
radon 50, 87
rainbows, dispersion 80
random motion 37, 39
react 42
reactants 25
reaction force 63
reaction forces 65
reaction rates 26
reactive 51, 54
recessive 13
rectangular glass block 79
reflection 78, 82
refraction 77, 79, 80
relative atomic
        mass, Ar 35, 46
relative formula
        mass, Mr 35
relative mass 41
reproduction 15
resistance force 66
respiration 7
resultant force 62
reverberation 84
reversible reaction 33
ripple tank 78, 79
rock and soil strata 18

rock salt 56
rubidium 51
rusting 24
Rutherford's scattering 89

S

salts 46, 52, 55, 56
sand 56
satellite transmissions 82
satellites 74
Saturn 73
scandium 49
secondary consumer 4
security marks 83
selective breeding 16
seriously easy 69
sewage works 7
sexual reproduction 15
shallower water 79
sharing electrons 45
sharp knives, pressure 70
shells 40, 42
silver bromide 55
silver chloride 55
silver halide salts 55
silver halides 57
silver iodide 55
silver nitrate 55
skin cancer 83
skulking cat 60
skydiver 66
slave piston, hydraulics 71
smoke particles 39
snow shoes 70
sodium 35, 44, 51, 52
sodium carbonate 35
sodium hydroxide 56
sodium ion 45
soggy pea 76
soil strata 18
Solar System 73, 74, 75
solids 37, 38, 54, 58
Sound 77
sound 84, 85
sound waves 84
southern hemisphere 72
Spanish inquisition 74
spectrum 82
speed 60-61, 68
speed of a reaction, 28
sperm cells 13
spying 74
squeaky pop 29, 52
stars 74, 75
state symbols 58
states of matter 37
steady speed 61, 62, 65
sterilisation 83
stilettos, pressure 70
stopping distances 67
strawberry 15
streamlined 66
submarines, pressure 70
sugar 31
sulphur 43
sulphur dioxide 9
sulphuric acid 29
Sun 4, 56, 73, 75, 87
sunbeds, uv rays 83
sunburn 83
surface area 2, 28
swapping electrons 44
sweating 2
symbol equation 59

symbols 58

T

take out the frogs 5
temperature 38
tension 65
the periodic table 47
thermal decomposition 32
thickness control 88
thinking distance 67
three laws of motion 62
thrust 65
timeless mysteries 40
titanium 49
top carnivore 4
total internal reflection 80, 81
toxic 29
transition metals 28, 46, 49
treatment of cancer 88
trends 48, 51, 54
tricky 58
trophic level 6
turn blue 34
TV and radio waves 82
twilight zone 72
twins 11

U

ultra-violet light 20
ultrasound 85
ultraviolet light 83
Universe 75
Uranus 73
uterus lining 22
UV rays 83

V

vacuum 39, 82, 84
vanadium 49
vapours 54
variation in plants and animals
        11
velocity 60
velocity-time graphs 61
Venus 73
vibrate 37, 38, 85
visible light 83

W

water 29, 33, 39, 52
water loss 2
wavelength 77, 79, 82
waves 77
weather satellites 74
weight 63, 64, 65
womb 22
work done 68

X

X-Rays 83
xenon 50

Y

yeast 31
yield 16
yip 87
yoghurt 31

Z

zinc 49
zygotes 13, 21
zymase 31